D1714095

A PERFUMED SCORPION

Contains the substance of lectures given by Idries Shah at universities in the United States of America, under the aegis of the Institute for the Study of Human Knowledge and the Graduate Institute of International Studies, Fairleigh Dickinson University.

Books by Idries Shah

Sufi Studies and Middle Eastern Literature
The Sufis
Caravan of Dreams
The Way of the Sufi
Tales of the Dervishes: *Teaching-stories Over a
Thousand Years*
Sufi Thought and Action

**Traditional Psychology,
Teaching Encounters and Narratives**
Thinkers of the East: *Studies in Experientialism*
Wisdom of the Idiots
The Dermis Probe
Learning How to Learn: *Psychology and Spirituality
in the Sufi Way*
Knowing How to Know
The Magic Monastery: *Analogical and Action Philosophy*
Seeker After Truth
Observations
Evenings with Idries Shah
The Commanding Self

University Lectures
A Perfumed Scorpion (Institute for the Study of
Human Knowledge and California University)
Special Problems in the Study of Sufi Ideas
(Sussex University)
The Elephant in the Dark: *Christianity,
Islam and the Sufis* (Geneva University)
Neglected Aspects of Sufi Study: *Beginning to Begin*
(The New School for Social Research)
Letters and Lectures of Idries Shah

Current and Traditional Ideas
Reflections
The Book of the Book
A Veiled Gazelle: *Seeing How to See*
Special Illumination: *The Sufi Use of Humour*

The Mulla Nasrudin Corpus
The Pleasantries of the Incredible Mulla Nasrudin
The Subtleties of the Inimitable Mulla Nasrudin
The Exploits of the Incomparable Mulla Nasrudin
The World of Nasrudin

Travel and Exploration
Destination Mecca

Studies in Minority Beliefs
The Secret Lore of Magic
Oriental Magic

Selected Folktales and Their Background
World Tales

A Novel
Kara Kush

Sociological Works
Darkest England
The Natives Are Restless
The Englishman's Handbook

Translated by Idries Shah
The Hundred Tales of Wisdom (Aflaki's *Munaqib*)

A PERFUMED SCORPION

'The Way to the Way'

Idries Shah

Whoever might perfume a scorpion
Will not thereby escape its sting
– Hadrat Bahaudin Naqshband, The Shah

ISF PUBLISHING

Contents

I Sufi Education

THERE IS A succession of experiences which together constitute the educational and developmental ripening of the learner, according to the Sufis. People who think that each gain is the goal itself will freeze at any such stage, and cannot learn through successive and superseding lessons. Jalaluddin Rumi put it in beautiful verse in the 13th century:

Man Ghulam i an ki dar har rabat
Khwishra wasil na danad bar samat
Bas rabate ki babayad tark kard
Ta ba maskan dar rasid yak ruz mard

'I am the slave of whoever will not at each stage imagine that he has arrived at the end of his goal. Many a stage has to be left behind before the traveller reaches his destination.'

We can run through a number of contentions about education as understood by the Sufis and represented both in their literature, in their stories and in their traditional ways of communicating materials and inducing experiences, to note both what is new and unfamiliar, and what may fall into the interstices of contemporary educational activity.

MONITORING BY THE TEACHER MAINTAINS PROGRESS

Time-lag between exposure to impacts and their absorption, together with the fact that people often 'abolish' the impact of a story by fending it off with a wisecrack or a riposte, may make acceptable social behaviour, but it can make for lack of sensitivity in the event. Attention to these factors is a part of Sufi expertise and care. The need to monitor one's own reactions, and to see why one is behaving in a certain way – self-observation without neurotic self-abasement – may be taken as the next important feature. Even at the very early stage of time-lag, wisecrack and self-study, we can easily note how difficult it is for some people to get the measure of what they are doing: how one may not know one's own time-lag characteristics, how one may wisecrack automatically, unable to control this response, how one may dive into an orgy of introspection. For this reason the monitoring of the Sufi teacher may be said to be so necessary as to justify the institution of teachership.

The attachment to externals, esteeming the container and not the content, is also a major human tendency, and a further explanation for the presence, or at least the effect, of the mentor.

BARRIERS TO LEARNING

The barriers to learning may be noted through illustrative stories or observed in oneself; secondly, they may be so ingrained through habit that there is a need for an operation of some kind, an exposure to an interchange, for them to yield. We have already noted that barriers cannot be dealt with by mechanical structures: by repeatedly telling people not to be subjective, for instance. This merely makes the determination not to be subjective ingrained as a characteristic in itself. It does not impart the quality of being able to do what one thinks one should be doing.

INDIRECT TEACHING

Indirect teaching, and the accumulation of a number of impacts or teachings to make up a single whole, is another feature of Sufi study. What is called in some disciplines 'enlightenment' can be, in the Sufi process, the result of the falling into place of a large number of small impacts and perceptions, producing insights when the individual is ready for them. The fact that one may be learning bit by bit, and storing up little pieces of information and experience which are, almost insensibly, to come together at some later date, naturally does not recommend itself to people who may be offered elsewhere something which, it is claimed, will give them instant insights. Hence the grasping for catch-all categories of teaching, which always claim to be comprehensive. Sufi study, therefore, cannot hope to compete with instant-illumination-offering systems, just as the much-vaunted nostrum called snake-oil will claim much more attention from some people than something less dramatic.

Yet the drop-by-drop activity of Sufism does cause a certain amount of restlessness, even among those who accept the postulates we have already mentioned. Hence it is often found that people complain that their studies are not proceeding along the lines they believe to be indicated: as in the case of the 'Tattooed Lion' story.

In this tale, from Book I of Rumi's *Mathnawi*, a man went to a tattooist, asking for the design of a lion to be tattooed on his back. But when he felt the prick of the needle, he cried out in anguish, asking the artist what part of the animal he was working on. 'The tail' said the other.

'Leave the tail,' cried the coward, 'and do another part.'

But when another part of the lion was started, the customer found that it hurt him just as much, and he instructed the tattooist to abandon that area, too.

This went on until the artist threw his colours and needles on the ground, and refused to do any more. So the artist had his wish, to leave off the work, and the customer had his wish, to be relieved of the pain. But the result was that nothing happened at all....

The foregoing questions, too, are tied up – in the educational event – by the problem of attention. People who have a portion of attention attached to something other than the subject under study will often, it is held by Sufis, be virtually disabled from absorbing the lesson. This has, naturally, been distorted into the claim that people must marshal and focus every iota of attention before they can learn. This is, of course, the doctrine of 'One aspirin will shift my headache, therefore a thousand of them will give me higher consciousness.' But the nature, quality and degree of attention is held by the Sufis to be as important as the more easily quantified input in learning situations.

Traces of this doctrine of a psychological mean, a movement between two extremes of opinion, belief or exercise, are indeed to be found here and there in Western literature, though seldom linked with any teaching situation.

People will campaign against immodesty with little result other than self-abasement, which may be worse when pursued in excess. As Shakespeare says:

'Self-love is...not so vile as self-neglecting.'*

OVERDOING THINGS CAN BE POISONOUS...

Short of the thousand aspirins, we can find almost innumerable instances of analogies (if not intended teachings)

* *Henry V*, II.4.74/5 (1598–9)

if we only transpose, for illustration, not necessarily for equivalence, into more familiar fields. I have just noticed a report to the British Royal College of Physicians of work done by Dr Elwyn Hughes, a University of Wales biologist. Massive doses of Vitamin C are believed to ward off the common cold. Dr Hughes took 350 people and gave them each 80 milligrams of Vitamin C, which is just over 2½ times the recognised normal daily requirement of 30 milligrams. These people contracted 18 per cent fewer colds during the infection season than the control group on 30 milligrams. There was a further group, given massive doses of over 80 milligrams a day. No doubt they got even fewer colds? Not a bit of it. Those ingesting over 80 milligrams got *no fewer* colds than the 80 milligram people. But they did get something else, continues Dr Hughes: the tendency to form poisonous substances such as oxalic acid in the body. Excessive use of Vitamin C, he says, could 'enhance the dangerous effects of some toxic substances already present in food'.*

Those who have seen the random application of supposedly esoteric practices on would-be illuminates in just such a mechanical fashion will no doubt note the almost uncanny parallel here.

FINDING FURTHER RANGES IN JOKES

When the other requirements are being observed, there are still more which have to be kept in balance. People who, for instance, are accustomed to hearing stories as something

---

* *The Times*, London: 24 September 1976, p. 14, cols. 5–6. Doses as high as 1000 mg a day have been suggested for colds....

to make them laugh, to inculcate a moral or to illustrate a point of doctrine, often find that they are unable to look and listen for other ranges of meaning in a story. They are described by Sufis as not learners at all, at least at that stage and in that condition. They are seen to be people who are attuned to moralism or jokes or dogma. This is why Sufis so often seem to be asking people whether they really are Sufi students, or whether they are in fact students of someone else, or something else. Sufis require attention to what they are teaching, in the spirit in which they are teaching it, no less than in the case of more conventional instructors. Similarly, people who come to consume, to be emotionally stimulated (whether by the presence of the teacher or the unfamiliarity and strangeness of the materials) are not students either, for the same reason.

NEGATIVE AND POSITIVE OPERATION

It might be said that people are always trying to test the genuineness of the teacher. But I have found more fake students than fake teachers!

Then there are those who, listening to what I have just enunciated, will say that we are harping on negatives and not affirming positives. They say this for the same reason as the others 'say' unconsciously what they do: by their reactions. If you have to fill the pitcher, the saying goes, you may have to empty it first. To claim that it should be filled regardless of what is in it, even if that thing is unsuitable, is to say something about your own lack of insight, not about the teaching or procedures.

HUMAN COMPLETION OR PSYCHOTHERAPY?

Sufi education is aimed at what the Sufis regard as the fundamental incompleteness of humankind in general. This means that the basic problem must be tackled, and not the symptoms. So Sufic education may be aiming, indeed *is* aiming, for this fundamental role, while the student (that is, the person who imagines himself to be a student) may be asking for psychotherapy, for secrets, for reassurance that his time has not been wasted, and so on. It is because the pitcher is already half-full that Sufis have to clear the way to understanding of these basic contentions before real teaching, as distinct from overfilling, can take place. This is not to say that the Sufi wants people to abandon anything which they already know. But it does mean that the Sufi must expect, as any teacher would in any field, that the requisite conditions for learning obtain. If the desire to oppose it, or the desire to consume it, are too strongly marked, there is little prospect of the learning process taking place at all.

SUFISM LEARNED BY MEANS OF ITSELF

Sufi study, too, is learned by means of itself, and rarely can even parts of it be approached through the individual claims of other formulations. It has its own postulates, some at least of which are not regarded as basic or even relevant in other systems. It is thus of the greatest importance that the student or observer of the Sufi phenomenon shall realise that Sufis do not teach in terms of other systems, however traditional or modern. Sufi work may verify and *illuminate* – say – psychology. We have yet to find that – say – psychology can produce a better way of studying or understanding Sufism and its teaching methods.

CULT-FORMATION AS AN ABNORMALITY

Failure to observe Sufic criteria in trying to learn, very much more often than not, will result in the oversimplifications which lead to a cult, or the trivialisation which leads to a vague religiosity, or in the intellectuality which leads to hairsplitting of an often comic kind. All these hypertrophies are well represented in cults and organisations, groups and writings which you can find all around you. I have already more than once publicly invited people to familiarise themselves with these materials, so that they might find out whether they can see things as we do, or whether they prefer the other, partial approaches.

HEMISPHERIC BRAIN-FUNCTION

An Eastern position on left- and right-hand brain function might well be that, however important these specialisations may respectively be, and however useful it can be to define them, there is yet another mode of cognition – though it may be connected with the interplay of the two.

On the subject of the two ways of thinking, Omar Khayyam (who died about eight-and-a-half centuries ago) might have been writing, in his poem about formalism and belief, when he stresses that both ways of thinking give rise to equally fallacious assumptions:

> *Qaume mutaffakar and dar mazhab wa din*
> *Jama'e mutahayyarand dar shakk wa yaqin*
> *Nagah manadi bar ayad zi kamin:*
> *'Ki 'eayy be-khabaran – rah na an ast na in!'*

People are thinking about creed and belief
All confused between doubt and certainty.

Suddenly a call comes from the Beyond:
'O uninformed ones: the road is neither this nor
   that!'

TRANSPOSITION OF CONCEPTS

You will observe, as we continue to examine examples of
Sufi thought in the educational area, how literal is often
deliberately transposed for figurative, and sequential for
holistic. I say deliberately, because this is not to be confused
with the ordinary process by which the one becomes the other
through misunderstanding or cultural deterioration. Among
the Sufis, the transposition is carried out deliberately; though
not as a matter of policy, only in response to situations where
there has been, as it were, a congealing of thought.

The Sufi teacher's perception of this is generally an inward
one, so that the examples which we choose as illustrations
are only the crudest – the ones which have aspects which
appear in physical encounters and verbal interchanges. And
it is worth remembering that this perception by the Sufi is
regarded by him as linked with a cosmic intuition, which
drives him to work in the field of human education of the
Sufic kind. In this feeling he agrees with Einstein that 'The
cosmic religious experience is the strongest and noblest
driving force behind scientific research.'*

---

* Quoted in his Obituary, 19 April 1955. This may be a driving force, but
   it certainly is not a discussable one: speech and experience have opposite
   characteristics. As Hujwiri, 1,000 years ago, quoting a Sufi director,
   said: 'To ask about experience (*hal*) is absurd, because experience is the
   annihilation of speech.' (*Kashf al Mahjub*, Nicholson's version, p. 370,
   1959 reprint. London: Luzac.)

AWARENESS OF MOTIVATION

For the Sufi in his area, as for the teacher in any more familiar one, a major consideration is whether the would-be learner is serious in his desire to learn, and whether he wants to work or play. He may be unaware of his own motivation.

TRUE AND FALSE TEACHERS

People are always asking how they can distinguish the true from the false among the swarms of Eastern sages competing for their attention.

One of the neatest and most enlightening interchanges on this subject I have ever heard is this one:

Someone asked a Sufi: 'How can I tell a true from a false teacher?'

The Sufi replied: 'I can tell you how to identify the false one.'

'Good,' said the other man, 'anyone who does not pass your test will be my master.'

'It is not quite as easy as that,' the Sufi told him, 'because you only have to find a supposed teacher who will accept you, as you are, as a disciple. This will be the ignoramus or the fraud.'

CONTEMPORARY PSYCHOLOGY

There has recently been a great deal of interest in relating Sufi knowledge to contemporary educational or psychological theories, and this continues. One of the advantages is that the literate public can, by this method, obtain some outside confirmation that Sufi teaching is authentic in the sense of being based on criteria which are verifiable by accepted methods of assessment. If a Sufi tale seems to show a knowledge of the lateral specialisation of the brain, this concentrates some people's minds wonderfully. They feel that 'Sufism must be genuine'. And it may, further, provide a framework through which some aspects of Sufism can be approached by those who need such reassurance. To the Sufi, however, the need for such activity is minimal.

CONSUMERISM IN APPROACHING KNOWLEDGE

Transpose it into a more usual mode: say, for instance, that people are doubtful of the advantages of a new commodity but can see how it would fit in with their existing lives by reference to established commerce, customs or preoccupations. Both they and the people representing the commodity would be pleased. But how far should either party go? Should the 'intending consumers' only concentrate upon the aspects of the new commodity which please them or reinforce their attitudes or ways? Should the introducers of the commodity put disproportionate effort into explaining these aspects, when the result might be to present the commodity inadequately, or occupy too much of one's time and energy? Again we have the matter of balance in where attention is put, and by whom. It is perhaps fortunate that the situation does not really arise, since it is our experience that Sufi teaching and learning does not need a hard sell or soft sell, but attracts a sufficient number and variety of people without having to enter into this kind of activity. But the matter should in fact be aired, because there are so many people who will insist on approaching the Sufi study in the 'consumer' way which I mention.

LIMITATIONS OF WORKING WITH DERIVATIVE MATERIAL

There is a distinct value in working with the spin-off from Sufi study. Certain stories and other secondary materials are of great interest to many people in psychology and education today. The materials are felt to be of value to individual disciplines, and no doubt they are. But the degree to which these derivative materials may be used for such secondary, or even tertiary, purposes really has to be explained. It would be inappropriate to suggest that people in the West imagine that Sufism is a mine of diamonds surrounded by much useless clay which the Westerner has to prise away. It would be equally unworthy to suggest that the contemporary Sufi is elitist about his Sufism. The truth, however, is that the Sufi aim is to Sufis fundamental, and the tradition and methodologies are intact and fully operative. Such room as there is for experimentation and 're-inventing the wheel' here is limited and limiting. You do not go to the Massachusetts Institute of Technology, for instance, for a device for frightening away evil spirits. Mismatching of ideas does not help anyone.

It is unlikely that people now being addressed include any who view Sufi knowledge as containing bits and pieces which could be picked up and fed into existing frames of education or psychology to give them a boost, and so I need not say much about such a primitive attitude towards what is, after all, among the most comprehensive and long-lasting – and versatile – traditions of man on record. The desire to acquaint oneself with the variety and sophistication of the Sufi approach, however, by means of *portions* of its instructional methods, is not the same as looking for fragments to loot them for repair work to an existing, perhaps experimental, structure. Sufis always welcome interest in their work which really is objective or altruistic, which really is educational or scientific. But, in order to familiarise oneself with the working of an elephant, grabbing the ears or tail will yield little enlightenment, commensurate with the energy employed, about elephants.

In Sufi education, therefore, focus, balance, the weight given to different impacts, experiences, the attunement of the learner: these are paramount, and the Sufi teachership mediates these elements.

HOW NOT TO LEARN

When any part of a form of learning becomes available, it is standard procedure in the human community, almost compulsive behaviour, that people pick up pieces which appeal to them, for vocational or psychological reasons, and charge off in all directions (like Don Quixote) bearing these pieces, which they then elaborate, simplify and proclaim to be the whole thing, and something to be urgently transmitted to all and sundry. Sufi studies are no exception to this. If you allow yourself to think, briefly, about what happens in familiar bodies of knowledge (say medicine, philosophy, social or even political ideas) you will see what I mean. The pattern is undeniable. Now, in most such instances, it is customary for an individual or a body of people to attempt to stop this process, or to regularise the situation, by forming a single authoritative institution through which the genuine materials or knowledge and/or practice can be regulated.

THE CIRCUSES

With the Sufis the matter is not so simple. With us, the cults are more publicly visible than the authentic teaching; the gurus are more advertised than the substance of the study; the transitional, superseded literature is more available than the measured guidance. The reason for this is that Sufism is in essence, in its more effective and truest form, too subtle, too delicate, too much based upon perception, to be expressed in the crude externals, the packages which people always at first demand of anything and which they are consequently widely offered by superficialists. This successive transition from the fine to the crude is characteristic of one way of the human handling of things, and there is little to be done about it. You can hardly deny that some clowns and circuses are Sufis and Sufism unless you can demonstrate *IN LIKE TERMS* something which is Sufism but which is authentic. Appreciation of Sufism is based on perception of it. Perception of it is different from a crude projection from it, appealing to logical or emotional minds. The onus is on the receiving culture to provide enough people interested on this level if the subtler reality is to find a means of harmonising with that culture. It is almost – but not quite – a case of people getting the 'Sufis' they deserve.

One of the most valuable remarks I heard during my youthful Sufi studies was this one, which yielded more and more as I contemplated it:

TEACHERSHIP IS FUNCTION, NOT APPEARANCE

'This visible institution of teachership exists in our dimension not because of the needs of the enlightened. It is there, to the contrary, because of the insensitivity of the ordinary person, who will not perceive what is there until this has been magnified into an external shape. Its first duty is to disappear from appearance, and to appear in real action.'

It seems equally possible to me that the new knowledge of the brain-hemispheres' operation may demand a similarly subtle institution to be devised for it, eventually.*

THE EXAMPLE OF CHRISTIANITY

I have recently noticed an interesting example of the deterioration of human beliefs, even in an area where there has been continuous teaching of specific doctrines for close on 2,000 years. A study carried out in Britain showed that, among Christians, while 70 per cent believed that there was a personal God, only 30 per cent believed that there was a Devil. Furthermore, only a minority – an average of 44 per cent – held that Christianity was a better religion than Buddhism. Among Catholics taking part in the same study, only 50 per cent believed in the Devil, while a full 92 per cent believed in an everlasting punishment in Hell. Again, in the same study, as a result of being asked factually verifiable questions as well, the research concludes that people believe more strongly in matters which *cannot* be verified than in ones which can.** From the total of Christian believers questioned, only one in three believed in human evolution....

Quite apart from several other matters which came up in that paper (published in 1962 and now quite famous), it surely is interesting to observe that the 'religion' of a large number

---

*   See Robert E. Ornstein: *The Psychology of Consciousness*, London and New York: W. H. Freeman and Company, 1972; and (second edition) Harcourt Brace Jovanovich Inc., and The Academic Press: London and New York, 1977.

** Brown, L. B.: 'A Study of Religious Belief', *Brit. Journ. Psychol.* 1962, Vol. 53, No. 3, pp. 259–272.

of religious people is at variance with the dogmas of religion which they profess, in spite of their having been exposed to its virtually unopposed specific teachings for many centuries, nearly 2,000 years. How successful is education?

If Buddhism is better than Christianity, why remain a Christian? If there is no God, how can one be a Christian? If there is no Devil, who is presiding over the everlasting punishment in Hell, how can Hell be something which is still believed in?

On what evidence, or by what process, are some of the Christian beliefs accepted and others discarded?

People used to quote 'I think, therefore I am',* but surely it is a matter of '*I believe it, therefore it must be so.*'

It is a Sufi contention that truth is not discovered or maintained by the mere repetition of teachings. It can only be kept understood by the perpetual experience of it. And it is in the experience of truth that the Sufis have always reposed their trust. Sufism is therefore not 'Do as I say and not as I do', or even 'Do as I do', but 'Experience it and you will know'.

MODIFICATIONS THROUGH IMAGINATION

The knowing, of course, has to be primary. Resorting to secondary renditions is all very well. But, as Rumi said, you cannot reach the milk by way of the cheese.

'Speak to each person in accordance with his understanding.' This aphorism used by Sufis bears study. The Sufi can only

---

* Cogito, ergo sum, of Descartes (1596–1650). Huxley showed that this phrase when analysed by Cartesian methods, really boils down only to: 'Something called thought exists'. (Huxley: *Descartes' Discourse on Method*).

teach where there is a public demand, as well as an external goal. The public can perceive the goal only when ready to do so.

It holds true in the teaching situation, where you can measure the understanding of the student.

But, such is the distortion of understanding in any general population, caused by the biases which cultures implant, and the programming and inflammation of the mind produced by so many pressures, that I feel we could modify this slogan in dealing with the general public to:

'Speak to everyone – they will modify it according to their imagination.'

It is often said that one should ignore obtuseness, and never tackle it head on, that by definition you can do nothing about it.

How convenient it would be if things were really as simple as that!

Experience shows that sometimes, at least, you must deal with obtuseness – otherwise it may indeed happen that obtuseness will deal with you....

If someone were to ask you what people it was among whom you would find Christians who believed that Buddhism was a better religion, that there was a God but no Devil, that concrete facts were less reliable than beliefs which could not be proved, and that there was no Devil but there was everlasting punishment in Hell, would you be inclined to think that it was in Britain?

SUFI ANALYSIS OF EDUCATION

After that gallop in strange but local country, we may return to our Sufic method of looking at education, as carried out by the concentration of indicated impacts. First I would like to summarise what Western people state education is. A recent study published in the United States* tells us that Western education may be split into three major categories:

1. The *indoctrination* system, which is generally called the transmitting of the values and disciplines of the culture to the next generation.
2. The *idealistic* system, which believes that what is inside should be allowed to come out; this has been called romanticism.
3. The *interaction* system, the most modern type, which stimulates the student and develops him or her by feedback; also known as progressivism.

The Sufi attitude to these three modes is that indoctrination alone is undesirable, that idealism may ignore that there are things to put in as well as to bring out, that interaction depends for its success upon a knowledge of what, when, and how to feed back, in order to enable the development, possession of knowledge and enrichment to take place. The interaction, which is closest to the Sufi attitude, demands that it be served by experiences which are themselves products of real understanding.

In their education, therefore, the Sufis operate a method of working with their pupils which is, because based on the possibilities of the situation, sometimes mystifying to observers. The theoretical approach, making people do things or learn things because this incantation is held to be good in itself, is probably very far behind us, though I cannot forbear

---

* Kohlberg, L., and Mayer, R., 'Development as the Aim of Education', *Harvard Educational Review*, Vol. 42, No. 4, November 1972, pp. 449–496.

from quoting to you the results of an investigation into an aeroplane crash as a consequence of the 'folklore' method of education:

A wide-bodied jet with nearly 300 passengers on board was coming in to land at Nairobi Airport, Kenya, one day, with a captain who had logged more than 18,000 flying hours. The plane was pulled out of its attempted landing when just within 70 feet above some rocks and scrub. It had been trying to fly *below* ground level. The captain had been with the company, one of the world's biggest, for 30 years. 13 per cent of captains in this airline, it is stated, have failed their jumbo training courses: the highest failure rate in the world. Other world airlines have averaged only 3.5 per cent failures. Investigations by their Airline Pilots' Association have shown that the course given to pilots does not actually *test* the ability to *fly* the aircraft, but it is heartening to read that 'the Working Party wants the exam to be replaced by a Company exam based on what pilots actually need to know to fly an aircraft'. As a comparison, the American airline United is quoted as having had only one failure to pass in 250 tests of pilots.*

Is modern education designed always on interaction? What are its sources and objectives?

Sufi education is based on Sufi knowledge. What interests many outside people, I fancy, and always has, is not so much what Sufi knowledge can be, but how it is that Sufis have so much knowledge of things which other people are concerned about. I have already said that the Sufi answer to this is that they get this other knowledge (recently noted in ancient Sufi classics are references to space-flight, power in the atom, evolution, time and space theory, navigable

---

* *Sunday Times*, London, 15 August 1976, p. 13, cols. 6–8.

balloons, sphericity of the Earth, etc.) as a by-product of what modern researchers would doubtless categorise as holistic or comprehensive mentation. At any rate, it is to us a by-product, however useful in our professions.

So when we talk of education, we must admit that the Sufis are fundamentally preoccupied with their own kind of knowledge. They are deeply interested in what other people call education, but this is mainly because, in a world where cultural transmission of information and abilities is the preferred method, the nearer people come to the truth about *ordinary* things the nearer they will be to the Sufi experience of objective fact beyond culturally transmitted experience.

WHO WOULD ADMIT TO IGNORANCE?

Saadi, the classical Sufi poet, in his *Rose Garden** makes a reference to this when he says that human ideas of knowledge are so fallacious that even if all conventional knowledge were to be removed from the world, there would not be one person who would admit to being ignorant. Saadi continues, in pointing out the educational problems of value-laden teaching, with a little aside about a Muslim and a Jew:

'To my amusement,' he says, 'a Jew and a Muslim were having an argument. The Muslim said, "If I lie, may I die a Jew!" And the Jew, with equal vehemence, swore that if he were to break his bond, he would wish to be regarded as a Muslim, like his despised opponent.'

It is on such murky pools as these, deeply filled with assumptions and conditioned bias, that people heroically try to erect educational structures. They will try, too, to produce

---

* Saadi: *The Gulistan*, 8th Book, Counsel 32.

or elicit, condition or cajole, out of them the more balanced, fulfilled, socially acceptable man or woman. The Sufis are not always popular for having said that for every person there are differing circles of belief: including those which are held by the surrounding community, and those which are known by direct perception. Or for saying that education should come from knowledge, not theory.

THE AIM

To help to provide people with the means to hold to the norms of their society while acquiring the understanding of a deeper truth, without either disturbing their own equilibrium or that of their society, is the aim of Sufi education. As one Sufi has said: 'If ordinary people, who admit the imperfection of their knowledge, can sustain society, how much more can the Sufi manage to retain his equilibrium, faced both with the principles of the environment and the knowledge of where it fits in with an Ultimate Reality.'

FLEXIBILITY

What the Sufis would regard as preparatory education, preparing people for deeper experiences as well as enabling them to fit into the existing society, involves above all a flexibility of approach which many people regard as inconsistent with ordinary life. That this is not so is amply demonstrated by at least a thousand years of connected Sufi history in the Middle East and Central Asia, in the Near East, India and the Far East: even at times in parts of Europe. So, first of all, I would list, as useful to anyone, the Sufi effect of familiarising people with concepts which they have not considered before. These are things which do not come into everyday life with the same sharp outline that the Sufis, through poetry, stories and other teachings, give them. An obvious example is to be aware that circumstances alter cases, and that things considered to be absolute for some purposes are only relative for others. There are innumerable examples in the stories which I have published. One Western thinker has noticed this problem and this need: 'Familiar things happen,' says Alfred North Whitehead, 'and mankind does not bother about them. It requires a very unusual mind to undertake the analysis of the obvious.'* We feel that such a mind is unusual only because human thought has got into a rut. This is one tale which has not yet been published: A camel and a mouse both happened to be opponents of what non-thinkers, mindless people, today love to call elitism. Each claimed that it should have what the other had, not something measured in accordance with a purported assessment of its requirements.

So water was given to each of them when thirsty, but both died. The camel died of thirst because it was given the mouse's ration. The mouse died of drowning when it fell into the camel's portion.

ASSUMPTIONS AND POINTS OF VIEW

This form of study involves, too, being able to see things from more than one point of view. Again, we have published extensively on this.

A third vital approach is to question and examine one's assumptions, without, however, becoming compulsive about it. In parts of the East, of course, people have adopted this

---

* Alfred North Whitehead, *Science and the Modern World* (1926), p. 6.

technique in isolation and so deeply that it gives rise to the sensation that nothing is worth doing at all – except, perhaps, examining assumptions. This and many other abuses are due to the employment of what are really instruments, not as instruments, but as holy writ or as magical spells. It is no different from repeating, say, the multiplication tables and expecting this to cause some marvellous multiplying effect. Indeed, the pointing out of the instrumental function in totems and formulae is a characteristic of Sufis. Some thinkers, of course, in the West (and even in the East) take this to such extremes that they regularly attract large audiences by declaiming at great length that people should not listen to teachers. The lesson is, therefore, that 'any instrument can become a totem, but few, if any totems, can become useful instruments – and then only when other circumstances are in alignment'.

SEQUENTIAL AND HOLISTIC THOUGHT

In terms of the lateral specialisation of brain hemispheres, I think we have an interesting illustration here. The linear item, say a phrase composed of originally semantically significant words, becomes a dirge or magical mantram, which is transferred to the mainly holistic hemisphere in the form of something not by then endowed with sequential meaning. A word becomes a form. There is a clue, perhaps, to what should really happen in the Sufi tradition that 'a word must have a sound, a form and a meaning, and they must all be appreciated together'.

It is certainly true that Sufi experience appears to make things which are perceived as ideas come into the field of action, and actions to prompt ideas. This may also be one source of Sufis doing things which have a physical shape but no verbal explanation, though they originate with an 'inspiration' and not in the form of words. It could even be maintained that Sufi education aims at getting both sides of the brain to work, and helping them to operate at times in concert, and not alternately.

Hence, we may say that: if the methods of Sufi learning were to be written down, the theory would be easier – but while *theory* becomes possible of understanding by this method, *Sufism* itself then becomes impossible to learn.

NARRATIVES

But a great deal of the Sufi teaching-in-action can be observed or deduced from narratives. While we can analyse many of these, it is lucky that they almost always have dimensions which mean that their entire versatility can seldom be completely rendered in banal terms and therefore worn out. Even some statements which have a crackerbarrel philosopher's application can also be used to expose the deficiencies of the aphorism when pushed beyond a certain unregenerate point. Take such a beautiful and arresting saying as one which is current now both in the East and the West: 'The journey of a thousand miles begins with a single step.'

When this is repeated enough, with the customary sage nod or clever wink, most people imagine that it is worn out, it becomes a truism. But when it is submitted for further examination, you may add to this something extracted from Sufi educational and psychological experience. This is to observe that, unless it is understood *how*, *when* and *where* to make that step, the assertion is devoid of the profound weight which casual and unthinking adoption so often ascribes to it.

Another thought, emanating from a state of deep contemplation, can be fed back into sequential terms and has been known to produce a useful capacity for learning beyond the obvious:

'If only he knew less – or more – he would be wise.

Of course, he would have to know it in a somewhat different way.'

SHIFTING OF ATTENTION

The shifting of attention from the expected to the unexpected is a technique which has some value; and it makes use, in Sufi circles, of conventions by violating them, to point to assumptions as to how a story will end and enable one to contemplate for a second or so peculiar possibilities:

A certain human being once found what he realised was a magical ring.

He put it on his finger, and, with the usual formula, said: 'Ring, do your work!'

In a twinkling of an eye, he found himself transformed back into the being which he had been before he had found a ring and wished to be – human.

Then there is a joke, which serves to see, sometimes, in a flash, how people are out of communication, and not in the way they imagine themselves to be disconnected, either:

The Minister of Health of a certain country sent a telegram to the Governor of a distant province. The message said: 'Shall we send you more doctors?'

The reply which came back from the yokels was:

'Send us less of the accursed magic spells which are smiting us with disease, and we won't need any of your doctors.'

There is another humorous tale which, among other illustrations, emphasises that people often think and act in isolation, not realising that this may sooner or later end in trouble, both in the ordinary world and in spiritual studies:

There was a countryman who had sold his watch because – he told a visitor – the trains ran on time within earshot and he therefore did not need one.

'But how do you tell the time, say, in the early hours of the night, when there are no trains?'

'That's easy. I have a bugle by my bed. When I want to know the time at night I blow it hard, as loud as I can, out of the window. Someone always shouts: "Who's that fool making such a noise at ten past three in the morning?"'

BASIS OF SUFI THEORY AND PRACTICE

Sufi knowledge is the knowledge of something beyond customary human perceptions, yet reached through the very world whose characteristics often stand in the way of such perceptions. This could well be a summary of the theory and practice of the Sufis. Seen in this way, something of a logic in one's approach may be reconstructed. I say 'reconstructed', of course, because from the Sufi viewpoint no argument or rationale is needed, no general theory of how and why one gets from A to B – because the Sufi knows about the A and B. The rationale exists for the benefit of those who may wish to approach the path but need a theory within which to do so. It might be noted, too, that by no means everyone demands such a theory. But the majority of people *do*, and the others will understand to whom one is talking, in this regard.

ENERGETIC ATTENTION

Even this coherent, linear thinker for whom we are, effectively, working, has to make a jump of energetic attention to grasp things which lie beyond the reach of his sequentially operating brain alone. His education has to take a new turn, when he is ready for it. This point comes, by the way, at the stage indicated by this interchange:

A would-be Seeker asked a Sufi:

'How long will it take me to arrive at the point of true understanding?'

The Sufi answered:

'As soon as you get to the stage where you do not ask how long it will take.'

This is not a conundrum; the Sufi, as I am sure you will realise, is merely saying, in a memorable way, that if your attention is on one thing, you will not be able to concentrate upon another. Learning, among the Sufis, requires attention to other things than 'how long things will take'.

Such ideas are not by any means unknown in the West. But they tend to be applied to the concepts of concentrated prayer alone, or of doing one's social duty; or heightening one's emotional pitch. The tradition of extradimensional perception being subject to specialised techniques apart from the moral and religious, however important these may be, is difficult indeed to find.

SUPERSESSION EXERCISES

Hence we see the Western convention in these words of John Donne, in the seventeenth century:

'I neglect God and his angels for the noise of a fly, for the rattling of a coach, for the whining of a door.'*

This is a small example of the possible use of things of this world, this prison of dimensions, to get beyond these

---

* John Donne, *Sermons*, No. 80, 1626.

dimensions. Oddly enough, it has often been objected that it is absurd to use something in order to transcend that very thing. Yet the smallest example from ordinary life will surely show that that is what we are doing all the time: with the Sufis, however, it is more strongly stressed that this is so. For instance, if you teach someone how to count, starting with piles of stones in order to end up with the relatively abstract Arabic figures, you may be said to have employed the concrete to get to the abstract, and to have used stones as something which you are determined to supersede.

If you do not do this, of course, keeping the constant awareness of the supersession factor in front of you, your learning system is in danger of becoming fossilised. You get conditioned to *stones*. The Sufi teacher's educational mission, too, is to work himself out of a job.

This brings us to the seeming paradox and source of great curiosity, the Sufi organisation and philosophy or ideology. The purpose of the Sufic learning-frame, whether it be a school, a body of literature or a set of ideas, is both to conduct one further and also to be dispensed with so that it does not become an end in itself. The visible cults which are well-known in the West are *degenerations* of learning-systems, and are those which have failed to observe this essential theory; and hence produced a grotesque.

ANONYMITY OF THE SUFI

Now we can explain why it is that Sufis hardly ever refer to themselves as such – it is so that the *word* should not become the substitute for the *experience*. Sufis, throughout history, have been known by so many names and styles that it even looks deliberate to outside observers. There are numerous different names for Sufi study centres, for the exercises, for the teacher and the learner. There are Sufi books which read like poetry, which speak of love or religion, which are full of stories or of theology, or even only the lives of saints. How, then, do Sufis know one another? Sufis just do: there is a link which needs no external object, not even a word, to maintain it. But how can we, the outsiders, it may be asked, know that all these people and all these artefacts, literature and so on, belong to the Sufi and no other tradition? Almost always because Sufis put in enough context, references to other Sufis, affirmations about Sufi experience, and so on. But there are many exceptions. For instance, although the major classics, which are numerous, are observable without doubt as Sufic, there are other books which only Sufis realise are Sufic in content and meaning.

The classic historical example of this is when the great teacher Ibn Arabi, of Spain, wrote a book – *The Interpreter of Desires* – in the 13th century. He was bitterly criticised for pretending to write spiritual materials while really wallowing in love-poetry. In a dramatic and historic inquisitorial event, Ibn Arabi himself interpreted the book, *The Interpreter*, line by line, to show his accusers the meanings in a religious sense which were veiled by his allegory, to their very great discomfiture. This is one of the most famous of all public Sufic teaching exercises. Since that time, informed people have been very chary of accusing Sufis of profanity, or even irrationality.

So the Sufi entity does not exist like the kind of agency we have for teaching other things. It cannot try to compete with the massive buildings of the law courts. It does not try to claim that its literature is invariably and literally true, irrespective of the state of the surrounding culture – rather the reverse. It does not deal in labels, at least not in labels which cannot be peeled off. The institution exists, but its cohesive force, the Sufi would say, is the knowledge which resides within it, which makes it exist far more permanently than bricks and stones, theories and other externals.

HARMONISATION

In order to *learn* from this institution, it is required that one *harmonise* with this concept. This harmonisation signals the entry of the individual into the learning situation.

The idea of teaching and learning among the Sufis is not always strictly similar to how it is understood in other systems. For example, few people would deny that if you are teaching a student, or trying to reach him or her, and his attention is on something else, the real situation is that no teaching or learning is in fact taking place at that moment. The student is absent in reality, though present in physical terms. In conventional schools, everyone knows this, but the fact is usually monitored retrospectively: by examinations, tests or performance. But for the Sufi the situation is everything. When you are not learning, you are not his pupil, and all responsibility towards you ceases for the period during which you have broken your contract. He seeks, of course, to draw this shortcoming to your attention, or to draw back your attention to the subject. And he tries to do this because he *can*: because, that is, he has (in the modern phrase) feedback. He realises that what he is teaching, which he feels he is conducting, is not finding a correct response. So here we have another peculiarity of Sufi learning. The concept that people's attention or receptivity may alternate in effectiveness is so much more than an observation, so different from a truism, that it is hard to describe it other than to use what is often thought today to be unacceptable terminology: he, or she, must be in *spiritual* contact with you, in order to know how to help your perceptions, and above all your understanding, to develop.

IMAGINATION

The importance of the spiritual contact has, rightly, been emphasised on many occasions. Naturally, of course, this has led to it being imagined to be the real secret, the only way, the thing which must be persisted in to the exclusion of everything else; so that we have very numerous people and organisations in all countries trying to establish and maintain this contact. The results of such lopsided efforts, of course, are to produce a large number of emotional or even sanctimonious people who *imagine* that they feel all kinds of things. They can usually be detected by observing whether or not they give *ordinary* people, those not interested in spiritual and esoteric matters, what is sometimes called 'the creeps'. If they seem weird, they probably are weird, not spiritual. Spiritual communication capacity is not to be grafted onto unsuitable bases.

Sufi knowledge is also imparted by exposure to those who have potential already. In detail, this learning is carried out by what we have to call both physical and 'electronic' procedures. But these are so many and so varied, and the very mention of them among excitable or impatient people causes so much emotional stimulus, that they are best left to the actual, not the hypothetical, teaching-situation. Traditionally, among the authentic Sufis, such studies always take place as a part of advanced and carefully ordered programmes, though some more visible and familiar circuses portray them as applicable to everyone all the time.

RITES, BELIEFS, PRACTICES

From the educational and general theory point of view, it is sometimes quite absorbing for a Sufi to look at the rites, beliefs and practices of many metaphysical systems and to note the stage at which the procedures have become ossified. How, for instance, sequences of words or sounds which were quite evidently once instrumental became invested with a holy or almost totemistic importance. How certain beliefs and even working hypotheses became structured into what is now thought to be legend or even literal historical truth. It is quite tempting to speak of this, even to publish on it. But there is a distinct disadvantage. Many of these schools or cults are social phenomena, strongly believed in by their adherents, who have more often than not stabilised their lives and their psychological equilibrium on the literal or allegorical truth of what someone else may see as vestiges, fossils, even, of a teaching school. To disturb such a situation can seldom have the kind of salutary results that some optimists might suppose. Apart from hostility, sheer depression can be caused. Quite often, too, nothing at all happens, as I remember from a small experience in Morocco....

THE EVIL EYE

My wife and I went to Morocco when she was expecting a child. She went into a shop and looked at kaftans, and very much liked one of them. The price asked was far too high, and so we left the shop, only to be pursued down the street by the proprietor, who was now trying to give it us for nothing.

I asked him why he should give it away like that.

'Don't you understand?' he shouted. 'What kind of people are you? A woman in that condition, when she covets something, puts the evil eye on anyone who doesn't give it to her! I don't want the evil eye!'

I said: 'That is absolute nonsense, and you know it!'

'I know it is – but what can I do? You see, I believe it!'

He knew, and he knew that he knew, but he was helpless.

I am not suggesting that the people who are wedded to such misunderstandings are entirely inaccessible. As long as the *true* facts about something are represented and available, there is always a chance, in fact a certainty, that some will appreciate them. But among the greatest discoveries of humanity, surely, is that it is surpassingly valuable not to mistake one thing for another. Among civilisation's greatest weaknesses, I believe, is neglecting this lesson in certain areas.

But I am not sure that if you can interest a murderer in mere robbery, you are really making progress in all useful directions.

* * *

The Sufi effort towards the acquisition of extradimensional cognition, in spite of all the qualifications with which I have been compelled to hedge its approach, can be seen in the specialisation of its attitudes. By this I mean that if you want to do something and you know something about it, you are often in a better position than a theoretician is to plan the approach to doing it.

THE DESIRE MATCHED BY THE MEANS

In the West, great advances of all kinds have been made (and we need not list them, for they surround us) by the application of certain principles. So it is with the Sufis. The difference in approach is the main easily observable distinction. A *desire* for something, however intense, is basic: but must, in both our attitudes, be accompanied by a *means* for obtaining or attaining it. That is how you produce great feats of engineering or physics. But if you approach extradimensional knowledge of the Sufi kind as a consumer or with too many assumptions derived from inapplicably different areas, at the best you will re-invent the wheel. That could take you centuries. So there are three approaches.

THE THREE APPROACHES

In order to select one of them, one must know what they are. Most people do not, in my experience. First, you can try to *force* your way through by sheer effort. Your experience in your fields and ours in our own shows that this does not work for less-crude ambitions. Second, you can imagine that you are learning when you are really only consuming or admiring or seeking attention: that is the behaviour of the cultist or ignoramus. Third, you can apply principles offered by those who are supposed to know something about the subject already. That is the way. Yet many of the people who want 'self-realisation' are not really prepared to adopt the methods offered. A delightful lady of my acquaintance who visited us recently said: 'If I don't get higher consciousness before I die, I'm going to be SO MAD....'

So, 'learning how to learn' is the Sufi answer, and it is observed by looking closely at Sufi ways of approaching things.

TWO WAYS...

One of these ways is represented in Sufi activity by inducing the individual's brain to balance itself so as to enable him to think as effectively about non-sequential things as about others. This is illustrated in a tale where the teacher, effectively, gives his pupil an exercise in thought which is carried out by attending to the seemingly inexplicable words which he says:

A man went to a Sufi and asked:

'What are the ways to greater consciousness?'

The Sufi said:

'The ways of Destiny and of Great Personal Effort.'

'And how,' asked the man, 'is the way of Great Personal Effort followed?'

'That is a matter to be answered in the Way of Destiny.'

Another important aspect of being able to learn from the Sufi orientation involves the *state* of the learner. If he is, for example, liable to react aggressively or masochistically, these barriers will tend to make it difficult for him to progress. Here is an instance of something which I myself observed.

THE FALSE STUDENT LEARNS HIS FALSITY

When I was young, I was sitting one day at the entrance to the meeting-place of dervishes where I was living. A man who looked like a wandering fakir trudged up to me and said:

'I want to see your Master.'

I went inside and told our teacher this, but his only words were: 'I refuse to see him.'

Rather nervous at having to carry such a message, I nevertheless did it.

The visiting dervish answered me:

'A Sufi cannot, of course, refuse to see a real Traveller on the Way of Truth. Yet your Master refuses to see me. It has taken this rebuff to teach me that I am not yet really a Seeker. In apparently being cruel, he has done me the honour of giving me a lesson. In being seemingly kind, by welcoming me and flattering me, he would have helped perpetuate my ignorance and self-love. I only hope that you, in your turn, will learn as much from this great man as I have today.'

It does, indeed, take a lot of learning, to differentiate within oneself between indulgent self-abasement and the humility without reward which enables one to learn. In a society where the refusal to see you is only interpretable as due to pressure of work or as a personal affront, it needs a lot of work on oneself. Yet when we say it takes a lot of learning, I cannot fail to observe that it is only a matter of *where* you put your effort. We have all seen people put more effort than is needed in Sufi study into willing a one-armed bandit to disgorge a jackpot of coins....

'COME BACK IN THREE YEARS'

On another occasion I learnt how one has to say and do whatever it is that will really help, not something from a book or a list of admonitions. I sat, once, with a sage who had received a visitor anxious to learn truth, and had told him to come back after three years.

I asked: 'Why did you tell him to return in three years?'

The Sufi said: 'My boy, worse advice he could have got anywhere: better advice he would not have taken.'

EXAMINING ASSUMPTIONS

I developed the habit of examining my assumptions without this becoming a compulsion through one phrase which I heard in a teaching-interchange when I must have been about twelve years old. This was when the Sufi said to someone:

'If you have to ask that question, you are not going to be able to understand the answer.' As time passed, I worked out how to formulate the questions whose answers might be useful to me.

An attitude which can seem perplexing but which trains the mind to be flexible without producing cynicism is another familiar Sufi preoccupation. One of my teachers put it in this memorable way to me, and I was able to use it as a framework through which to approach many things, including the very many changes in life and circumstances which befell me:

THE UNTAUGHT AND THE WRONGLY TAUGHT

'Hindsight,' he said, 'shows how often yesterday's so-called truth may become today's absurdity. Real ability is to respect relative truth without *damaging* oneself by refusing to realise that it will be superseded. When you observe that today's controversies often reveal not relevance but the clash of the untaught with the wrongly taught, and when you can endure this knowledge without cynicism, as a lover of humankind, greater compensations will be open to you than a sense of your own importance or satisfaction in thinking about the unreliability of others.'

The assessment of the relative importance, or value, of people and situations, or components of a situation, in regard to their learning function, is a further Sufi specialisation. In other words, things which happen in everyday life may or may not conduce towards learning about humanity and about extradimensional reality. One can become aware as to which of these are useful by having allegories or paradigms which recur, and which are recalled to the mind and form a guide. One example is contained in this story:

THE WISE MAN AND FOOLISHNESS

Two men were fighting when a wise man came along.

One of them ran off in a rage, and the other said to the newcomer:

'I have been practising placidity and calm for many years, and I am regarded as a religious man. And yet that man, who has become angry, calls me a fool. What good will that do him?' 'Ah,' said the wise man. 'If *you* are a fool, perhaps by tomorrow when his temper cools *he* will realise that it is vain to argue with fools. But if you *are* a fool – tomorrow you will almost certainly still be one, in spite of all your experiments in placidity. But *he* will have learnt something.'

It will not have escaped your notice that I have been moving from one illustration to another without necessarily linking the two; that we have alternated arguments and verbal statements with tales and imagery; that stress has been placed upon allegory and imagery within a sequential narrative which is not, however, expressed in historical, personality or logical terms for very long. I have chosen this method of approaching this subject in order to attempt the switching of attention which is characteristic of the Sufi literary techniques of stimulus and what is technically termed 'scatter', to give you a glimpse, in twentieth-century terms, of the atmosphere and method of the classical books of the Sufis of the past. I have, of course, changed the allusions to local matters – such as those of thirteenth-century Persia or the tenth and eleventh centuries in Central Asia, and I have provided examples of subjects of present-day concern, and I have also made other changes, in order to offer stimuli – and the lack of expected stimuli – analogous to dissertations of those ancient times.

This process, in turn, the medieval Sufis developed out of the earlier frameworks which they adapted from the centuries before them; because it is the constant updating of the literature and approaches to specific audiences which most characterises Sufi activity. This involves, as you will have seen, a method of dealing with materials which is not entirely uninteresting and is certainly selective of materials. But the selectivity is of a *different kind* from that to which we are accustomed, where, perhaps, the intention is artistic, or didactic. The selection in this case is made to offer a kaleidoscope of impulses, some of them familiar, some of them intended to encourage interest, others to stimulate disagreement. But a major intention behind such materials is to enable the reader or hearer to observe his own reactions, as well as merely to react or to memorise.

It is amusing to record that this technique, so easy to observe when one is on the lookout for it, has so confused and so often annoyed scholarly, 'sequential' no doubt, analysts, that they have had very hard things to say about it.

'CHAOTIC' LITERATURE

In the case of Jalaluddin Rumi's *Mathnawi*, written in the thirteenth century, literary and Orientalist specialists delight in describing it as chaotic, running off at tangents, being emotional rather than logical, full of information interlarded with tales and stories, and derivative because it is replete with quotations. Yet the *Mathnawi*, though not understood by everyone, is still regarded as one of the world's literary masterpieces and by Sufis as a textbook of their schools. Its contemporary value has, of course, been reduced by the fact that present-day readers do not subscribe to all its postulates, and because one needs a Persian cultural background to make full use of its dimensions.

Coming as I do from a culture saturated in the *Mathnawi*, even *I* had to be coached by my teachers in the parallels to Rumi's thirteenth-century concepts before I could make the transition to the Central Asian mentality of my early years. Naturally, nobody less than a major poet could today produce anything as compelling as the form and content of the *Mathnawi*, but its Sufic 'scatter' plan can nevertheless distinctly be observed and reproduced in a manner adequate for other cultures in continuing its educational work.

DISCONTINUITY

Perhaps the greatest heritage of Sufi thought, if we are to review both the literature and the actual Sufi school methods, is the establishment and maintenance, in writing and action, of the principles of flexibility and *discontinuity*, though not at the expense of adequate lucidity and the capacity for sustained thought.

This seems to be nothing less than adding an extra 'switching' mechanism to the established ones. By this I mean that we are all familiar with the process whereby our thinking is, so to speak, *switched* by others and by outside impacts.

We call this the effect of emotion, or the driving force of logical thought, according to the kind of thought which is uppermost. We are also aware of what might be called *deliberate* thought: when we decide to think about something, either sequentially or holistically. From the latter concept we tend to assume that *all* our thought is controlled, or that if it is not, it is rightly uncontrolled. Who, for instance, would like to do a kind action as a deliberate decision? It has to be produced by some 'other' impulse, something outside our control, for us to accept it as real.

But the relative weakness of the ordinary, untrained consciousness in being unable to switch itself off and on, to deepen itself, or to hold certain ideas in abeyance, is seen to be weak when we observe how individuals and numbers of people are played upon, diverted and pulled along channels chosen by others, sometimes acceptably, sometimes otherwise. Among the Sufis this is regarded as lack of concentration, or incomplete mentation. It is, I believe, only those who have *not* experienced this who tend instantly to imagine that directed thought, directed by oneself to a far greater degree than is usual, would be sure to sacrifice 'something else'. This cannot be preached as a doctrine, since when rendered in mechanical terms such as those which I have to use to get this down on paper or into relatively coherent verbal terms, it sacrifices the element which gives this experience its sublime and liberating life.

Alas, at a juncture such as this, when one can only speak to a limited extent about things which do not belong to the area of speech, one realises why, to the fury and bafflement of others, so many Eastern thinkers have to content themselves with saying such things as that:

'Whoever has the skill to fashion precious jewellery also has the ability to hide it effectively from thieves.'

And there is an even harsher saying that a moment of truth is of little advantage to whoever needs a good half-hour of it.

But we can take consolation for the future in the Sufi teacher's somewhat negatively expressed piece of advice, which yet carries within it the instructions as to what one should do next in order to learn more:

'Do not be that person who puts a *grain* of rice into a pot with the expectation of drawing forth a *handful* of food when it is cooked.'

THE VISITOR FROM SPACE

I am quite sure that there is a very useful and quite unusually fruitful collaboration in the making between Sufi thought in its designed expression and the large number of people in the West who will accept that to them unfamiliar systems may have to be studied by unfamiliar methods. There is a discernible groundswell of opinion which does not want to be sidetracked by cults or satisfied with gimmicks. The first step forward from here is connected with the level of understanding.

A colleague of mine in the Middle East emphasised the need for mutual understanding when we met recently, and contributed this very modern Sufi-type tale to submit to you, as a warning that we should not miss this opportunity of communicating as the people in the story did:

Scientists from this world had positioned a satellite to broadcast a call to any passing interplanetary being, to show that there was intelligent life on Earth. The apparatus was linked by a translation computer which was designed to put the visitor's words or signals into English.

Sure enough, before very long a superior being on a space mission came across this device. Recognising it, he dismounted from his ship and spoke into the apparatus. He said: 'Earthlings, I am a superman, out of Space....' As the automatic translator began to type out this message, the scientists on Earth were hopping up and down in excitement. But the phrase 'Earthlings, I am a superman, out of Space....' was printed out, due to a lack of harmony between the vibrations of the two parties, as 'People of dirt, I am a virile heterosexual, without an apartment....' So the message was interpreted as a hoax, because it was too trendy, and apparently nonsense, by the serious Earthmen. And the Spaceman: well, he was rather too serious-minded, too. He decided that as there was no reply the satellite must be broken, so he fed it to his space-cat.

II On the Nature of Sufi Knowledge

THE DISCIPLE WHO BECAME A TEACHER

Once upon a time there was a Sufi exponent who possessed a really enormous range of teaching-stories, of accounts of the doings and sayings of the classical masters, and of the knowledge of how and when these elements were to be applied in the learning situation, to provide the real psychological effects which otherwise run away, as you know, into the sand.

On the basis of the learning-by-contact theory, this teacher always allowed a certain number of less-able pupils to attend his seminars. Among these was one man who never got anything right. When the master asked for an interpretation, his understanding was faulty. When a story was being considered, he would ask irrelevant questions. When the community was set a specific tale to study, he would choose a different one, and so on.

At long last, and quite reluctantly, the master told him that he must go. After all, although a student who is unable to learn may provide an example of teaching by reversed behaviour, there is also the maxim: 'A dog will not improve a pool of rosewater.'

The student was, naturally, upset, but eventually, noting that the teacher would not change his decision, he packed his few belongings and sorrowfully went on his way.

Two or three years later, this same Sufi master was sitting at the entrance to his home, when a magnificent, chauffeur-driven, custom-built limousine, gold-plated and upholstered in antique silken hand-woven rugs, swept up to him. Out jumped the unsuccessful student, with his hand outstretched, beaming joyously at the sight of his old master.

The sage beckoned him to sit beside him, and said:

'I am glad to see that you have become successful in the world. Am I to take it that you have at last given up the desire to penetrate the meaning of the teaching-stories?'

'Oh, yes,' said the former disciple, 'I certainly took your advice to heart. Instead of studying them, I *teach* the stories now...'

Now this is a very old story; so that, if we can talk of a fresh adaptation of the Sufi materials to a contemporary community, we must also note the persistence of certain standard patterns from early times right up to the present day. You might be quite surprised at the number of supposed teachers (who have appointed themselves) who winced when we made certain materials available. The same sort of pattern is seen, too, in the individual who imagines that he can teach himself beyond a certain point. People read stories, or ransack books for Sufi exercises and psychological or spiritual techniques, and then they, remarkably often, set about trying to put them into practice. Now, imitation may be the sincerest form of flattery, but who wants to feel flattered by the sight of someone deliberately attenuating his or her own capacities? And, above all, using materials with a developmental function to do it with? It is, almost exactly, paralleled by the accounts of people who want to get thinner but eat such large quantities of special slimming foods that they ingest more calories than ever – and get even fatter.

Well, it is for this exact reason that the Sufi study methods monitor the progress of the student, in order to discover whether there is still an underlying hankering after extremes. This is why the negative requirements of the Sufis are just as important as the positive ones. You cannot graft religion on greed, for instance, otherwise you only get, at most, greed for religion. The best that you can do is to introduce certain beneficial experiences alongside the detrimental ones, so that the one, in comparison with the other, will be seen and felt to be preferable.

MONITORING AND FRESH ADAPTATION

The 'fresh adaptation', of course, must take into account that some of the Sufi concepts and practices which we have observed to possess the most useful and thorough effects are ones which do not automatically fit in with various major Western preoccupations. This does not mean that Western people cannot embody them into their tradition: or that they are totally absent from the culture – indeed, I have seen the transition effected supremely well. But it does involve the addition of a dimension which we can call flexibility of attention: always verifiable by experience, but not often instantly acceptable as logical or necessary.

TEACHING VERSUS ENTERTAINING

If you want a little example of the cross-purposes situation which can occur when people from one culture meet those from another, there is the incident which I observed which shows how people who want love and attention think that they do not, and that there is some other motivation for a contact:

I was sitting with one Sufi when a foreign visitor, dressed in what he and his associates imagined to be a 'spiritual seeker's' garb, came rushing in. 'Why,' he cried, 'don't you let me see you more often, Master?'

The Sufi looked at him, wearily, 'Because I am trying to teach you, not to entertain you!'

The last section in this present treatment contains over fifty separate remarks about Sufi psychological practices: and a number of these, of course, take time and reflection to digest. Above all, they need to be studied both in isolation and also in the kind of comprehensive context which has been provided for them by Sufi workers throughout the centuries, in Eastern cultures largely; and by this I do not mean by dabbling.

THE RIGHT TO BE SERVED, NOT THE RIGHT TO DEMAND

The 'naturalisation' of these elements is a microcultural endeavour which takes time to organise, let alone to spread throughout a whole people. It is worth remembering that the basic study on how to do this has already been done by those Sufis whom – it will be recalled – it took no less than four to five centuries finally to implant it in the East, with the psychological victory of Al-Ghazzali in the twelfth century.*

The integration of this way of thinking, which has its own symmetry, requires, then, the ability to think and work along lines which are established by the teaching itself. Please note that I say 'the ability', and not 'the compulsion'.

Learners under a compulsion to learn make poor learners, in Sufi estimation. Teachers cannot teach by imposing anything.

---

* See my *The Sufis*, New York: Doubleday 1964 and London (W. H. Allen, Octagon Press and Star Books, 1964 and 1977); London: ISF Publishing, 2014.

As Maaruf Karkhi, the Sufi and disciple of my own kinsman, the Imam Raza, said over a thousand years ago: 'A Sufi has a right to be served, but he has no right to demand.' It was in this connection that, a thousand years later, my great-great-grand-father, the Jan-Fishan Khan, said: 'If you want to be owned by a tyrant, accept someone who only imagines he is a pupil.'

First of all, we must note the argument that there are two kinds of teacher: the familiar type, who feels a need to teach, which is often referred to as a vocation, a calling. The second kind, the *Sufi* teacher, has had, initially, a stronger thirst to *learn*. When this thirst is assuaged, he is then in a position to tell whether he should be a teacher or not. Those who act on behalf of Sufi teachers, administering – as it were – their prescribed courses, are not teachers but channels, though they may sometimes be learners at the same time. The distinction may seem subtle to those not accustomed to it, but in practice it becomes completely clear. 'Patience is the food of understanding.'

Second, there is the avoidance, without hypocrisy, of outward show and not to demand more immediate satisfactions than necessary from involvement in the Sufi enterprise. This practice, and the reality of its sincerity, are normally made possible by attunement with a Sufi teacher. Without the permeation of this characteristic among the participants, the Sufi psychological climate does not develop. People who believe that they only have to appear sincere to be sincere, cannot learn anything from Sufis while they remain at this stage. The special atmosphere produces a quality of what people sometimes call 'transparency', and which can never be counterfeited, and which needs no spiritual perceptions to perceive. It is never found in the absence of sincerity, though it is often imagined to be there by those who are themselves subject to deception. It is sharply to be distinguished from the sententiousness and dealing in platitudes and vague generalisations which are so often imagined to be 'spirituality'. Referring to this quite inevitable quality, one commentator has remarked: 'A (Sufi) saint is holy until he knows that he is.' Self-conscious goodness can never be real goodness.

In more compressed, almost mnemonic, and more conventional form, the two factors have been referred to as aspects of patience and modesty.

Third is the ability to act or not to act, in accordance with what one knows by experience to be a required mode of action. This is the stage of action stemming from unconcern for superficialities. It is the condition of doing something, or nothing, not because it is expected of you, but because it is the real thing to do or to avoid. The reason why some Sufis require their disciples to wear identical robes is to signal that they have *not* yet reached this stage, to assert that they are still at the point where appearances are important to them. Those people who assume a certain kind of identifying garb – and we have them in this society in plenty – especially the ones who imagine that the dress is connected with psychology or religion – are in fact, in Sufi symbolism, asserting that they have *not* surmounted this barrier.*

To be at the stage of unconcern for appearances is not the same as the deliberate adoption of untoward behaviour. But the 'contrary to expectation' conduct and words which are attributed to so many Sufis are traceable to the working of this characteristic, and also to a lot of their innovative and perceptive mentation on lower levels, too; for it indicates the absence of hampering assumptions.

---

* 'The Teacher gives up outward appearances for inward reality. The Seeker at first adopts robes and rosary, then as he progresses he gives up ceremonialism and adopts real devotion.' *Irshadat-i-Shaikh Ibrahim* (Persian MS of the famous Sayings of the seventeenth-century Ibrahim Gazur-i-Illahi).

Inwardly, this condition is that of the sovereign individual, whose perceptions and understanding, not rules or dogma, motivate him or her.

The Sufi student is always encouraged to act in accordance with social norms*, but also to practise 'listening' to his intuitive sense in the attempt to perceive whether this or that word or action was indeed correct in a wider context. If he is, for instance, prompted to alternative action, he can evaluate its reliability by reviewing his day's life in retrospect. The success of this monitoring will depend on its frequency and honesty, but will be clouded if it becomes obsessional.

In Sufi understanding, the analogy of someone not being able to perceive inner dimensions of reality in ordinary life is that of people who look at familiar things and still do not notice what they might mean. Our technical term for this is 'heedlessness', and the equivalent is of people in day-to-day matters who become unaware of some things of importance going on because they are thinking about something else.

In a somewhat responsible – as distinct from an irresponsible – exaggeration, we have a small story which aims at fixing an analogy for this in the mind.

SEEING AND UNDERSTANDING

A King was once becoming impatient with a lecture by a Sufi, and made up his mind to score a point or two off him. Thus it was that, as soon as the Sufi had said, for – it seemed to the King – the thousandth time that 'hundreds were blind and even those who were not blind could not understand what they saw', he held up his hand.

---

* Saadi: 'The Path is not otherwise than in human service.'

'As King of this country I insist that you match allegation with demonstration. On pain of death, *show me* these people who are blind, and those who are not, but will still not understand,' he said.

'Certainly, your Majesty,' said the Sufi. 'And I will give even you, a mere king, the honour of taking part in my demonstration.'

'What do I have to do?' asked the King.

'You will sit for one day in the bazaar, the local market, in your robes and wearing your crown, hammering upon a brass tray.'

And so the King sat there all day with the Sufi beside him. Every few minutes someone stopped and asked, 'What are you doing?' and the Sufi, sitting nearby, took down his or her name.

At the end of the day the Sufi said: 'Your Majesty – here is the list of all the people who stopped and were so blind that they could not see what you were doing, hammering a brass tray, and had to ask.'

The King was quite impressed; but then a thought struck him. 'Yes, but what about a list of the people who are *not* blind but still cannot understand what they see?'

'That's easy,' said the Sufi, 'all you have to do is to make a copy of the same list and it will do just as well.'

The condition of the modern world, I sometimes feel, thanks to mass-propaganda, is such that, if the child in the crowd of the fable were to cry that the Emperor had no clothes on, almost everyone around would hush him; he would be sent for psychoanalysis, and an explanation would be found for his 'disturbed behaviour'.

Fourth in Sufic psychology, in what we might call 'awareness of reality training', is the ability to switch attention. This has to be achieved so effectively that, for instance, one can identify with and detach from another person so completely as to feel and see as if one does it by means of, or through the other individual. From this exercise have developed, as you may imagine, many examples of thought-transference, which often decimates the ranks of the learners, who run after this as if it were their golden key. Because it is a lower-level acquisition which, employed prematurely, inhibits further understanding, this exercise is never allowed until the learner has first developed quite unusual capacities of responsibility.*

As ESP of this kind is seen as a by-product which syphons off what is referred to as a subtle transformation energy, to misuse it is inappropriate. This 'attention-switching' is probably one of the procedures which are used in magical and occultist ambition, because it can undoubtedly be cultivated: though when practised in isolation from a wider context, it withers and dies remarkably quickly.

Fifth is the sensing of the relative characteristics of people and situations, in order to be able to assist in the harmonisation of these and other elements to help enrich all the participants in cognitive capacity. Since Sufi learning, for all practical purposes, takes place among people grouped in a special way so as to reinforce one another's abilities, this understanding is very important. The analogy might be, if we were to say that there were eleven people with a productive capability of 10 volts each, linking them would produce 110 volts, which could in turn illuminate a light bulb which would enable *all* of them to read a page of a book featuring vital knowledge.

People collected at random, or merely because they want, for group-mentality reasons, to enrol, cannot in Sufi tradition

---

*   *Cf.* Idries Shah: *Oriental Magic*, London 1956 etc. (Octagon and New York 1973: E. P. Dutton Inc.); London: ISF Publishing 2015; and Idries Shah: *The Secret Lore of Magic*, London 1957, 65, 69, 71 etc. (F. Muller) and New York (Citadel) 1957 etc; London: ISF Publishing 2016.

form such a learning group, again for all practical purposes. Sufi harmonisation takes place at a much more sensitive level than merely collecting what are sometimes called 'like-minded people'. The Sufi statement here is: 'Every gathering of people has its own potential. Those collected arbitrarily have only physical, mental or emotional potential.'

Sixth comes the cultivation of service without the sensation of reward, either expected or gained. This practice, according to Sufi psychology, stimulates the perceptive capacities in a manner which is impossible when they are blocked by the cruder emotions engendered by enjoyment of – or even anticipation of – reward. If you do a good deed – and why should you not? – and you feel gratified – and why should you not? – you have already been 'paid' by this very sensation. There is no further advantage coming to you, according to this psychology. 'Indifference to reward' is the short title of this capacity.

These six formulations are, of course, carried out by prescription, not by adoption; the learner being assigned exercises by the teacher or his deputy, in accordance with what the pupil can do at the time. Since the ordinary level of human life and action depends so much on such things as appearances, objects, clothes, looking outwardly and not inwardly, having attention directed and not directing it, even thirsting for ESP, looking at the surface of situations and not for an inner content, wanting to teach, acting whether one needs to do so or not, grouping people just because they want to be grouped – and so on – it is not surprising that people do not just stumble across Sufi perceptions. Given this situation, it is even gratifying that they should wonder at all whether there is any other way of approaching really sensitive perceptions than their everyday one.

Many other exercises, of course, *do* exist, and all of them depend for their success on monitoring feedback.

THE QUALITY OF UNDERSTANDING

All this may seem tiresome, compared with the garish appearance of the imitations. But the Sufis say: 'Burglarious attempts on the House of Knowledge will in the end only earn you a bite from the rats in its basement.' So there is no alternative in fact – only in folklore and imagination.

A favourite Sufi quotation: *Tukkalimun nasa ala qadr uqulihim* ('Speak to people to the extent of their understanding'), involves the whole question of the *quality* of their understanding. If they have *supposed* 'understanding' of psychology or anything else which effectively prevents a wider understanding, more preparatory work is needed.

Another Sufi speciality worth noting is summed up in the phrase: 'Always be careful to make a *bad* impression on undesirables.' Remembering this often helps one to interpret otherwise baffling behaviour by Sufis...

The six formulations just given accord very closely with our assessment of the dominant thinking of wide areas of Western culture, and cut right across the systems of belief which people *themselves* imagine divide them so sharply. As an instance, let us take people who hate money and want to change the social system. They will be just as wedded to wearing special clothes, essentially uniforms, to display their allegiances as are the people who hate *them*, love money and want to preserve the social system. People who crave attention will be just as likely to fix upon one kind of psychological or other system to be their panacea as another. When you demonstrate or assuage this craving for attention, the symptom – attachment to a panacea – will often disappear. So *we* are really interested in fundamentals, not in appearances. Is there an equivalent response in the other party? – In the candidates for this knowledge?

The conventional methods of assessment in this case accord very closely with our intuition on the state of the culture under examination. We may say that we 'just feel' what people are like and how they might be taught or how they prevent themselves from learning. It is almost equally interesting to me to review the materials which have been fed back from the publication of our books during the past twelve years.

LEARNING PROBLEMS INHERENT IN CULTURAL PRIORITIES

We have collected just under a quarter of a million letters and other communications (actually 240,000-odd) during this period: over 70,000 of them from the United States. The points I have dealt with crop up again and again as explanations for the questions, and account for success and failure in understanding the materials. We now have a mosaic picture, as if built up by these responses. Interestingly, after the first 1,500 letters, no essentially new queries appeared; ideas and opinions just repeated themselves, in one form or another. Thus, only three-quarters of a million out of 35 million words contained points which had not come up before. We were able to gauge by this feedback, too, the interestingly comparative rarity of the appearance of some ideas which were sometimes quite commonplace to *us*. We certainly gained a mosaic picture of how people here think, and what they think about, what they know and what they have not troubled themselves to learn.

Our correspondence with scholars, and conversations carried out with people who did not know of our main interest (shall we call this the 'control group'?), showed that the 'esotericist' correspondents did not differ from the academic, the psychologist or ordinary people-in-the-street in terms of blind-spots and other basic characteristics. This is an indication that perhaps *all* groups, though notionally approaching things from different points of view (and believing that they have very different orientations one from the other), display a similar, *deeply basic* pattern of preoccupations and motivations. Ambition, interest, failure to observe, and so on, may *seem* to be rooted in the vocation or major interest. In the testing, they are seen rather to be inherent in the cultural priorities. All cultures specialise and neglect, include and exclude. It is fascinating to note how people imagine that to accept certain postulates must automatically make them avoid others, however.

After all, if you talk to someone who believes that success only comes through a prodigious expenditure of effort, and that success is what everyone else also thinks is success, you can hardly expect him to be interested in the possibility that there can be non-energetic success and non-ambitious progress – let alone the contention that what everyone else may be thinking might just be incomplete.* The farthest you are likely to go, without the kind of extensive explanation I am giving you, is to say that, once upon a time, effectively everyone believed that the Earth was flat or that mushrooms were produced by lightning. All this has been somewhat encapsulated in the reputation I seem to have in the media for saying that we tend to live in pessimist cultures, because I pointed out that the members of these cultures believed that if they followed *some* principles of their heritage, these automatically excluded others. Since people can't easily refute this, they over-simplify it into 'Shah is that man who

* And let alone non-energetic progress and non-ambitious success…

says we're all pessimists.' Although it *is* the twentieth century, it is perceptibly a trivialising society we live in.

The rationale for all this is, of course, not hard to see. It means that a culture will be based on certain assumed absolutes, and that it is these which inform – and sometimes restrain – the products of the culture, whether they be individuals, institutions or schools of thought. Cultures are not changed, or even necessarily enriched, by changing their appearance. They can, however, be *invigorated* by filling some interstices with possibilities for enlargement of the individual which do not in reality conflict with basic postulates; or which enable the premises to become more flexible. It is in understanding that such *imagined* 'absolutes' are somewhere flexible that this kind of development can in fact take place. This does not need to happen to everyone; and, indeed, applied to all purposes it would be absurd. But there remains the fact, in psychology as in physics, that something which acts like an absolute for some purposes may not do so for another. After all, many people know that all straight lines are really curved (Einstein) but in most usages this information is not required.

The very basic needs for reassurance and rapid identification – the labelling – of people, as instances, are useful in any culture at a certain stage of its development, or for some transactions; as they are useful for any individual or animal for some purposes. Institutions supporting these needs will tend to come into being anywhere. They will both provide these desiderata (there are many others one could think of) and also create a further demand for them.

People who do not want so much reassurance and identification, for some reason, will not necessarily appear in particularly large numbers, since the production of more and more of the type in demand will generalise and sanctify, as well as deeply root and institutionalise, the whole mechanism.

Institutions which offer reassurance and identification will continue to appear. Unless their true inner dynamic is noted, they will, of course, continue to be perceived by people of that culture as whatever their outward shape says they are. Anyone or anything which *seems to say* that such things are of no use, or of limited use, as steps upwards, even, will then seem to be a threat.

THE PURR AND THE SNORE

So we cannot blame people for looking for what they have been trained to look for: rather than for what *may* be there, but which has few immediate emotional stimuli or other short-term gratifications to offer.

You may have heard of the 'Cat and Snore' experiments.

A recording of a cat's purr was played to random collections of people. Those who were told that it was a human *snore* really disliked it, and turned away in disgust. Those who were informed that it was the purr of a contented cat (apart from those who disliked cats) expressed a desire to hear more. When snores were played, in recording, to an audience whose members had been told that they were an amplified recording of a kitten purring, everyone present expressed pleasure: except, of course, those who did not like cats.

It is because people's assessments of all kinds are so subjective and also very dependent upon suggestion and assumptions, that one has to be sure – *before* giving them study materials – that they can make some use of these apart from the use which they may expect one to lay down, or which is automatic because of their assumption-habits.

It is not an accident that the word 'egregious', though according to dictionaries it is not value-loaded, is almost always seen to be employed as a pejorative. 'Egregious' – 'out of the flock...' Is humanity a flock of sheep? Only if they want to be, or are trained to be.

If Sufism is a road, this is the camber on it. It certainly explains the difficulty in establishing in people's minds the reality of things which may be every bit as important, as valuable, as useful, as those on which they have built their current interests. It is as simple as saying that you can sell the sizzle of the steak easier than you can sell the steak itself.

Sufi teachings, though we will get to the more specific practices later, have to be remembered as being 'performed' as much as they are spoken or explained. Now, the built-in bias in the human mind says that if something exists, it can be explained, and should be, but only in the terms of the hearer. Well, what happens when we say that something is 'performed' as much as 'explained'? The same bias says that 'performing' is something like theatre: or that it is auditory, tactile, visual – even olfactory if you like – art. So, in no time at all, all jokes are Sufi jokes – all music has inner meanings; all movements or 'dance', once performed, shall be held to be significantly performed for spiritual or psychological purposes even if in reality only mechanically repeated. Because some Sufis have – rarely – used music to encourage certain states in those who might need them, all Sufis must, of course, be musicians. Because there was once a Sufi 'dance', the Sufis are dancers: and people who watch or take part are participating in 'Sufism'. Now all this is, of course, just as true – and as false – as to say that television is the test card you see on your TV screen. Look at things this way and you have nothing to lose but your cargo cult.

One must beware, then, of this extravagance; this proliferation of things, based on the unconscious assumption that 'excitement must be meaningful' – it has to be the right kind of excitement.

PROLIFERATION OF EXTERNALS

The proliferation of externals, and the taking over of one thing until it claims to be the whole, are continuously warned against by the classical Sufis, and the need for these strictures is equally obvious today. 'If the scissors,' said our great teacher Jami in the fifteenth century, 'are not used daily on the beard, before long that beard will, by its luxuriance, be masquerading as the hair of the head.'*

So Sufi studies and development always have to be approached through the awareness of an underlying flexibility and sophistication. Sufi teachership is the method for maintaining this consistency without mechanicality, this specificity of real humanitarianism without mawkishness, this effectiveness without that very same camber of assumptions taking over...

It is almost entirely because the human being's every interest is ordinarily stabilised on what Sufis regard as secondary matters that people have virtually no prepared ground in which to observe and experience something more subtle. So they recoil from such phrases as the supposedly perplexing

'When not-being is clarified in the Essence of Truth,
The secret Treasure becomes manifest.'
(*'Adam dar dhat i haqq chun bud safi / Az u ba
zahir amad ganj i makhft.'*)
Shabistari, *Secret Garden*

---

* Jami, *Baharistan* ('Abode of Spring'). This tendency – to mistake externals for centrality, and to be excited by superficials whose characteristic is only raw stimulus – is well described by the critic Benny Green, writing about the same problem in another area. He calls it 'a distillation of all the peripheral idiocies with none of the great central ennobling factors'. (In *Punch*, 3 May, 1978, p. 750.)

Yet even when put into words, the state referred to here is remarkably accurate in this rendition. What prevents people, under ordinary circumstances, from understanding it is not that it refers to an altered state of consciousness which they have not known; but, in our experience, because their minds are cluttered and they don't know how to stand aside from this clutter.

As I was casting about for a relatively unhackneyed example which might illustrate, here, the selective-thinking effect of the obsession of people with immediate interests, something quite dramatic and entirely suitable for the purpose suddenly descended on me.

The telephone began ringing, with calls from, it seemed, all over the world. Journalists were insisting upon my telling them whether the International Monetary Fund, then meeting in Manila, would grant Britain, up to her ears in debt, the nearly four billion dollars she was desperately in need of.

Slowly I disentangled the reason from their continuous questions. Dr Johannes Witteveen, Chairman and Managing Director of the International Monetary Fund in Washington, and a man of great distinction, is on record as being a Sufi. So, it seems to follow, I either know about what he is going to do about Britain, or – according to more than one newshawk – I am in a position to tell the Director of the IMF what to do, or may indeed already have issued my instructions...

Almost immediately after this came an article in a British national daily newspaper, with a four-million readership, in which I am quoted as influencing Dr Witteveen by something I said about Sufis and achievement on BBC television. But who are these Sufis? We learn from the paper that some of them must be pretty crazy, since one (said to be a professor) threatened to put a curse on a journalist; but (and I quote) 'Still, the news that the boss of the International Monetary Fund is a believer gives a strong "credit rating" to the

He called his sycophants together and said, 'I have this great idea. There is this hospital corridor with this beautiful girl being wheeled down it, strapped to a trolley. Camera tracks to operating theatre, where this evil-looking surgeon is bending over her…' The sycophants chorus, 'Great, Boss.' 'Well,' he says, 'there's just one detail I want you fellows to iron out: what kind of business is this guy in?'

A SCHOOL AND A LEAVEN

The Sufi entity is a community and an organism which is neither a tribe or nation nor an indoctrination machine. Its function, as a school and a leaven in societies, is what has enabled it to develop and flourish again and again in the most diverse cultures. It is worth noting that although *all* Eastern people may seem to be the same to people in the West ('all Chinese look the same to me'), their traditions and attitudes vary so very much that there are far greater differences between, say, an Indian and a Persian than between a Frenchman and an Italian. But Sufi enterprises have been as much subject to decay and to distortion as has any other human activity.

The fact that human systems are subject to deterioration, because of human psychology, of course, as good as imposes the requirement that this change in emphasis and the restoring, reviving function of the Sufis should always be a large part both of their capacities and of their concern.

The sheer deterioration in information alone leads to vital elements in traditions being lost, where there is no deep insight. Though I do not suggest that what I am about to tell you is a frequent happening, it certainly does show you what can happen:

A London journalist telephoned the United States Embassy there to ask that the Gettysburg Address be quoted in full to her. 'The information man pondered,' she records, and then he said: 'Is that a *public* office or a *private* residence?'*

Sufi knowledge is cultivated in its study-format, often known as the Tariqa, the Path, whose activities can be called the 'Studies *in* Sufism'. It is also disseminated through the literary, scientific, cultural and other established institutions of the day in what might almost be called a department, which we could term 'Studies *of* Sufism'. It is, too, in operation through ordinarily unidentifiable areas of human life in the field which some have called 'associated activities', and which we may term 'Studies *for* Sufism'.

This situation can be rendered quite adequately in the form of a diagram. It is the secondary materials, however, which, for the most part, are the subject of attention by scholars. The reductionists use these, too, and also borrow some exercises and externals from the first department, and base their simplistic 'Sufism' upon these.

Once one has a grasp of this diagram, it is relatively easy to identify most forms of what is described as Sufism, and to know what their stage of development is.

PERCEIVING THE IMITATORS

The ultimate solution will be when the people interested in the field will read enough of the materials to be able to perceive the inadequacies of the imitators. So mass reading materials, tape, lectures and so on not only provide the shams and the self-deceived with a means of contacting others and of maintaining cults: they are open to be employed to increase the flow of legitimate information and knowledge.

* 	*The Director*, London, May 1973, 'Point of Information'.

On this latter basis the research and proper progressing of Sufi learning can take place.

This is another area where we have found a value in people's having access to a great deal of material and forming conclusions from it. When people read our books, parts of which are designed to give them many aspects of the same thing, reflection of the holistic kind does seem at times to enable them to grasp something of what we are doing which is deliberately not written down sequentially. When, as often happens, they look at our work and also at that of others, and allow their overall consciousness to scan it and digest it, they seldom appear afterwards to find so much value as before in the work of those whom we refer to as fragmented.

So the linear method may be useful in acquiring materials: and the other method, perhaps employing the right hemisphere of the brain, might integrate materials so as to provide reliable guidance for the individual. Of course, the student must be aiming for more than a magic key to be able to profit in this way.

When I published, in 1964, the book entitled *The Sufis*, one distinguished literary reviewer (Professor D. J. Enright, in *The New Statesman*, 25 September 1964) said that it was a success, though by definition a foredoomed failure. In saying this, he was referring to the fact that holistic experiences cannot be described by linear methods, but that a certain kind of 'scatter' technique used in that book, by giving glimpses, and deliberately refusing to follow through with too great systematisation, was actually able to create a non-linear impression. What is interesting to me (in addition to the fact that there were even then people who saw what was being done), is that when I quoted this review at the time, people furrowed their brows and seemed not to be able to imagine what a 'success of a foredoomed failure' might be. Since, however, the research about the two sides of the brain has become relatively well known, the reverse reaction is more common. Now it is easy to find well-read people who *do* understand the reviewer's remark. And that has all happened in a decade or so...

I must admit certain exceptions, where people have come to a clear understanding of the intention of 'operational literature' in spite of the scholastic bias against something they merely want to interpret, not to use. A good example is the article in *The American Scholar*, no less, which stresses the fact of *The Sufis* being written on the principle of the 'scatter method', and notes that 'people who aren't flexible enough to read differently can't profit from it'.* Such a statement, appearing in a journal of this prestige, naturally caused a lot of fury, but it must have needed editorial courage to print. And, incidentally, it had taken no less than six years for this new information from the ancient East to penetrate into this medium.

This all means, of course, that we have a contemporary language in which to talk. So long as the language does not take over and make everything reducible to a two-brain or 'scatter' theory with no further dimensions, we are greatly enriched in our communications capacity by this research and recognition. When some people, including highly esteemed spiritually oriented thinkers, try to put their reactions to some of our materials into conventional words, they almost despair. The Reverend Eric Wild, editor of a highly thought of Christian journal, meets the challenge like this: 'cease to be content with the review and turn to the book' – he is reviewing my *Wisdom of the Idiots* – 'Buy, beg or borrow the substance instead of skimming the pallid shadow. I warn you, though, after reading the book you may shut it: and, like

---

* 'The Sufis', *The American Scholar*, Spring 1970.

the rich aristocrat, be filled with a sadness because of your attachment to a superabundance of conventional wisdom.'*

So we can get some idea of the extent of this enrichment if we note what our previous vocabulary was like. If I were to talk to you in pre-two-brain days, I would be expected to speak only logically and sequentially, in a disciplined manner, proving my arguments, moving from A to B, and so on. The only terminology to put up against, or beside, this would have been arty-crafty, or airy-fairy, which is far too limited for us. Or, perhaps, we could have spoken vaguely about '*real* experience', or 'something which cannot be described, because description means limiting…' Literature now being read is still loaded with this kind of talk, and probably will have to rely on much of it for some time to come. But even 'experiencing something whole', lacking the dignity of a physical organ or mental mechanism to which it could be assigned, was, not so long ago, equivalent in many people's minds to sheer hocus-pocus. All the words are there, in the dictionary, and they do not really help at all, for they are linked with what we can now call unfashionable, even inefficient, certainly limited formulation: words like inexpressible, undefinable, incommunicable…

You can have a lot of fun, by the way, with dictionaries and books of supposed synonyms in this connection. I note that in one such bible of the English language we have, listed under 'unintelligibility', the words incomprehensibility, doubtful meaning, perplexity, mystification and transcendentalism. We can fathom the mind of the compiler when we see, equated with *unintelligible*, the word *undiscoverable*, and with even 'incomprehensible' and 'insoluble', 'impenetrable'…But, since

---

*   Rev. Eric Wild, 'Sufficient Wisdom', in *The Inquirer*, London, 12 December 1970, p. 3.

'unambiguous' and 'legible' are also placed almost together, I suppose we must make some allowances for this particular thesaurus of words having been written by a calligrapher or pedantic drudge, rather than a man of other kinds of learning...

We can take cryptic utterances, formerly admired for their mysterious quality, and see that they might well indicate an awareness of two different modes of operation in respect to the same material:

SEEING AND KNOWING

Ibn Sina, the great philosopher, met the Sufi Abu Said.

When they were asked to comment on the meeting, the philosopher said of the Sufi: 'What I know, he sees.'

The Sufi said of the philosopher, 'What I see, he knows.'*

Here, surely, we have the two forms of awareness: the sequential knows in one way, the holistic knows in another – the way called here 'seeing'.

So it is with the nature of Sufi knowledge. This knowledge, in its real form, can be provoked and cultivated – given the existence of certain key factors. It cannot be described; neither can it be called impossible to communicate, nor can it be watered down. Yet these are the three forms in which people try to offer it to you. In the form in which it is *known* as Sufi consciousness and yet appears in the shape of wise sayings and interesting information, it is a secondary product, and really requires a different word to convey what is meant by it. But this secondary material, correctly used, is of the greatest possible value to the provoking of Sufi understanding. Most

---

* The Sufi Abu Sulaiman rightly wrote: 'When the self weeps because it has lost / The essence laughs because it has found.'

people make the mistake of learning the secondary material: which is rather like memorising the form or appearance, the weight and size, of an instrument, instead of learning how to use it. We, on the other hand, only know the how and why, and leave the size and weight to others.

Sufi materials, when employed by Sufis, bridge the gap between the inexpressible, holistic experience and the working of the hard-and-fast, obvious linear mode. They do this by the operation of the Sufic system of learning. Ask any Sufi what the use of the experience is, and he will say that it is the Sufi organism which enables people to 'return to the world', to relate the holistic experience to their human life and their being.

This is clearly enough noted by Jalaluddin Rumi himself, in a collection of Persian poems (Shams-i-Tabriz):

> Every form you see has its essence in the Placeless
>   [he says]
> If the form goes, no matter, for its origin is
>   everlasting...

Everything on Earth, as Rumi said, exists because it has an origin in another dimension, where that thing is perfect, where the multiplicity of forms is understood – not only perceived – as a unity. This is why, of course, Sufis regard things 'of the world' as being valuable to help towards the experience of the absolute and understanding its meaning. Any greater interest in the phenomenal world is regarded as prone to develop into a form of idolatry: the technical term used for fixations and conditioned attachment. The automatism of the assumption-system...Sufis diagnose as fetishists those religious-minded people who worship the externals of religion, or who are conditioned to respond only emotionally and without advanced perception to religious formulae. The arguments of the classical Sufi masters on this point (and they are the direction in which to turn for reliable information on it) are still unsurpassed. Sufi exponents have always been clear-minded enough to understand how even some of the most sublime of human thoughts have become – through misuse or over-use – 'veils', as they call them, barriers actually interposed between man and subtler things.

THE RELATIVE AS A CHANNEL TO THE TRUE

A major element of the Sufi position, therefore, is that there is an Absolute from which ordinarily perceptible things may be termed a local and inferior, incomplete concretisation. To attach oneself to these secondary things, beyond their due role as preliminaries, inhibits progress towards perception of this Absolute. Yet an understanding and employment of the possible role of the secondary things makes possible the progress towards the Absolute. This is encapsulated in the Sufi aphorism: *Al mujazu qantarat al Haqiqat* – the Relative is a channel to the True; generally – less accurately – translated as 'The Phenomenal is the Bridge to the Real'.

The stimulus of the holistic mode of the brain, achieved by those who perceive how, when, where and with whom this is to be done, is part of some of the Sufi knowledge procedures, where another part may be considered the application of stimuli deriving from the other side of the brain, the sequential side. The need for avoiding the over-concentration of intellectuality and also too much stimulus of the emotional, may even be taken, at times, as cultural and technical analogues of the preferred operation of the two cerebral hemispheres.

So the Sufis do not claim to be great intellectuals, and they certainly do not pose as gurus or intoxicated mystics:

except sometimes to illustrate the limitations of these. They do not even claim any exclusivity in what they are or what they do. And this certainly does create havoc when people are told it. As a sidelight, it is interesting to note that people are so unaccustomed to this middle-way approach that some earnest enquirers become quite affronted when told that we are *not* involved in proving our superiority or in knocking the other fellow's product.

There is, of course, only a limited audience for someone who says: 'I am an expert only in my own field. I have an intact and working tradition. If you are interested, I will show you something of it. If you want assurances that you might join a special and superior group through us, you have, for us, the wrong attitude, and we cannot do business.' Western people – and a good many in the East as well, wedded to more didactic and less truly education-oriented ways of thinking – still show real astonishment when they hear the standard Sufi statement, as for instance voiced by Sheikh Abdullah Shattar, who used to say, in India in the fifteenth century:

> Please show me your spiritual attainments, to share with me – if you have any. Alternatively, you are welcome to share *my* knowledge.

That is our approach.

Interestingly enough, we are now able to assess the state of mind of the commentators on so-called mystical systems and religion, by the relative weight which they put on one or other mode. The extreme scholastic will be wedded to the sequential, and the almost entirely 'inspirational' personality committed to the holistic. Faced with Sufi materials which alternate specifics with love-poetry or exposure to sounds and colours, for instance, these two types of thinker show their characteristics quite dramatically. I have, for instance, been more than once delighted to note that two reviewers will take a book which I have published, and provide us with what each imagines to be a balanced review, when what they *actually* show is a reflection of their respective right- or left-brain biases. Hence the *same* piece of literature will be characterised by the one as 'too sterile and intellectual', and by the other as 'airy-fairy experientialism'. This is only possible, of course, when information about the effect of the two biases upon opinion has not yet filtered down into general knowledge, and eventually reviewers like these will no doubt have to modify their behaviour to become, or appear to be, objective: but this will be when they catch up with the scientific work. In the meantime, they can be part of our illustration material...Later, their work will become a part of history; a warning, even.

The insulation of the two kinds of brain operation which occurs in societies where there is no real bridge between them, where vocations are divided according to whether they are intuitive or logical, may actually produce a society in which two lots of people cannot talk to each other. Worse, they might talk, but be unable to understand one another. Worse still, they can think that they *do* understand, but are not likely to understand.

ADVANTAGES FOR SUFI KNOWLEDGE

Analysed from this point of view, there are two possible advantages for Sufic knowledge:

- Firstly, that what scholars have taken as the incoherence of the Sufis and other mystics may have a newly perceptible rationale.

- Secondly, that the deterioration of so-called mystical systems into right-brain and left-brain specialisations alone can *actually* be monitored by a study of the existing practitioners, and the way opened to a not disreputable study of the alternating techniques of those Sufis who have maintained, for at least ten centuries, the concept and the operation of the bridge between the two modes.

As soon as word of the new and powerful approaches you are now hearing about gets around in metaphysical circles, you may expect many people to 'discover' or to 'reveal' this as part of their 'teachings', so I advise you, if you are interested, to investigate what these same people thought about the matter before there was a two-brain bandwagon to get onto; or an assumptions framework; or an objective view of Indian guruism – or even a Sufi non-lunatic, pedantry-free approach.

In the meantime, there is a little story about how the 'mystic' sees both the right-brained dreamer/romantic and the left brained scientist/literalist, as part of the same kind of person:

A wise man once said to a scientist: 'Which do you believe: that a primitive creature, over millions of years becomes a man, or that a frog, instantly, becomes a prince?'

The man of science was indignant: 'What kind of a person do you take me for?' he asked. 'I know what kind of a person you *are*,' said the Sage, 'but I am just trying to establish your opinions on yourself.'

III   The Path and the Duties and Techniques

GREAT PUBLICLY KNOWN Sufi teachers, those who can operate within *all* the concepts which might be necessary for comprehensive school work, are extremely rare, appearing about once in a generation. We see this if we look at the prominent ones of the past thousand years, and distinguish between such figures and those with merely local or keeping-the-tradition-going competence. I have listed, in *Tales of the Dervishes*, only forty-five of them in the last millennium; which is about one in a generation. The medieval dervish textbook *Awarif al-Maarif* (the Gifts of Knowledge), which covers about seven centuries, gives about half as many – equivalent to one for every forty-four years. And Aflaki, the biographer of Rumi, lists the first seven masters in Rumi's spiritual pedigree as living through just over two centuries, which makes one teacher every thirty years.*

Al-Ghazzali, both revered by Christian divines of the Middle Ages and regarded as a standard Sufi authority since the twelfth century, has codified, as it were, some of the characteristics of Sufi learning and teaching in a manner which has not been excelled.

---

* Idries Shah: *Tales of the Dervishes*, London 1967, 219ff. (1982 edition); the *Awarif al-Maarif*, Calcutta, 1891; *Acts of the Adepts*, 133–5 (Redhouse's translation, London 1881). Reprinted as *Legends of the Sufis*, London 1976, with a Preface by Idries Shah.

In his *Revival of Religious Sciences*, an enormous tome not yet fully translated into English, he addresses the would-be student with the phrase:

> He who knows, and knows that he knows, follow him.

The next three dicta in this vein, often distorted into popular jingles, are in reality precise, technical aphorisms, and he quotes them from Al Khalil b. Ahmad (when he is referring to the teacher) whose duties are three:

> He who knows, but does not know that he knows – he is asleep: wake him;
> He who knows not, and knows that he knows not, he wishes to learn – teach him;
> He who knows not, and is ignorant that he does not know – reject him.

The Sufi's competence does not extend to those whom the culture has still to affect to the limit of *its* own ability.

THREE CAPACITIES: GHAZZALI

Three capacities, Ghazzali continues, go with Sufi knowledge:

1. The power of extra perception, consciously extended;
2. The ability to move bodies outside their own mass;
3. The capacity to acquire, by direct awareness, knowledge otherwise obtained only through much labour.*

---

* Ghazzali: *Kimia Al-Saadat* (Alchemy of Contentment).

The duty of the teacher is, notes Ghazzali in his *Book of Wisdom*, that 'he shall not withhold any advice needed by the student; neither may he allow him to try to reach any stage until he is able to master it, or to permit him to attempt anything intricate until he has perceived the simple things which precede it...' [You can't get very far with someone who takes a prayer book back to the book shop 'because it doesn't work'!]. He must make sure that the student realises that this knowledge cannot endure together with competitiveness, boasting or a desire for power in respect to it.* The protection of knowledge, affirms Ghazzali, from those who might distort it, is more important than teaching itself. And the operation of teachership is so important, as Aflaki notes, so vital that a learned man who does not act is – effectively – an ignoramus [*Munaqib*].

There are many characteristics of the teacher noted by this standard author, but the Duties of the Student are those which tend to interest newcomers to this field. There are ten of them:

THE TEN DUTIES OF THE STUDENT

The first duty is that the student must make himself inwardly clean. This means that he must be able to operate without the distorting effects of anger, greed, envy, and so on, which are not really regarded by Sufis as human, but rather as pre-human.

The second duty is to have worldly interests, but only to the extent that they are needed by the *social* environment.

---

* Ghazzali, *Kitab Al-Ilm* (Book of Wisdom).

The watchword here is that 'Knowledge gives nothing to a man until he gives everything to it.'

The third duty is of complete submission to the teacher. This is, of course, part of a contract of mutual and total respect. Ghazzali illustrates this with a story about a time when the secretary of the Prophet Muhammad was about to mount a mule. Ibn Abbas, a member of the Prophet's family, came forward to hold the stirrup. The Secretary said: 'O Cousin of the Prophet! Do not trouble yourself.' Ibn Abbas answered: 'We have been commanded to treat thus the Wise.' Then the Secretary kissed the hand of Ibn Abbas, saying: 'And we, too, have been commanded to revere the Apostolic Family.' Knowledge cannot be attained except through humility. This relationship is quite different from the guruist submission system.

The fourth duty is not to concern oneself with apparent differences in formulation and opinion of the various studies. The student must follow and acquire the form which is that of his teacher.

The fifth duty is that the student should familiarise himself with areas of laudable knowledge, apart from his own field. This is because knowledge is interrelated, and because ignorance of other branches of learning so often produces bigotry and scorn.

The sixth duty is that the student should study whatever he is following in its due order. Sufi knowledge is the most advanced knowledge, it is noted here. It is quite different from mere repetition and assuming various beliefs handed down by one's predecessors. This is as true in religion as in anything else.

The seventh duty is not to approach one part of study before that which comes before it has been completed. This is because each stage prepares for the next.

This caution about doing things in the right succession can be illustrated by the tale of the illiterate peasant who learnt to read. Someone stopped him in the street and said: 'Well, friend, I suppose you're reading the Bible now?' 'Bible?' demanded the peasant indignantly, 'I got past that months ago. I'm on the horse-racing results now...'

The eighth duty is to understand the relative ranking of the various studies. Inner development, for instance, is higher than those studies which do not deal in human durability.

The ninth duty is that the aim should be self-improvement, not visible power, or influence, or disputation. Neither should one *despise* such external studies as are carried out by others, which might include law, literature and religious observances.

The tenth duty is to know the connection between the various studies, so that one should not concentrate closely on relatively unimportant things at the expense of perhaps distant though significant ones. What is *really significant* is of *real* importance to the student.

THE STATIONS AND THE STATES

Now we may turn to the exercises and the concepts which surround them. First of all there is the *Station*, called *Maqam*. This is the word for the quality which, at any given moment, the student is cultivating, under the instructions of his director. He may be expected to stabilise himself on, say, *Taubat* (turning back, repentance) until his teacher assigns him to another developmental exercise. It is a posture, and so is termed 'an act'. In one sense it is a 'stage', a word which has also been used for it.

But a Stage is not a *State*. 'States' are episodes of altered consciousness which come upon the individual without his

IDRIES SHAH

being able to control them. The 'State' is also known as a 'gift'. The main objective of Sufis experiencing these flashes is to get beyond them. The eminent teacher Junaid of Baghdad emphasises that 'States are like flashes of lightning: their permanence is merely a suggestion of the lower self.'* This means that their filtering through the unaltered ego causes delusions. If they can be felt, and are valued instead of conducting to the stage of perceptual breakthrough, the student is in a rut.

Being in one or other 'Station' is seen as a sort of necessary bondage, part of the training of the Commanding Self, and a time comes when this is no longer necessary. Similarly, the 'States' indicate a contaminant in the person, who should instead (and eventually will, it is hoped) experience knowledge instead of intoxication or dazzle. The passage in Hujwiri's book, the first one in Persian on Sufism, goes like this:

All the Teachers of this Path are agreed that when a man has escaped from the captivity of Stations, and got away from the contamination of States, and is liberated from the abode of change and decay [dependence upon time and place] and becomes endowed with praiseworthy qualities, he is disjoined from all qualities. That is to say, he is not held in bondage by any praiseworthy quality of his own, nor does he care about it, nor does it make him conceited. His state is hidden from the perception of intelligence, and his time is exempt from the influence of thoughts.**

* Quoted by Hujwiri, in the *Revelation of the Veiled*.
** Hujwiri: *Revelation of the Veiled*.

The Sufi director knows by the behaviour of the student what the condition of his secondary, 'commanding' self is at any given time.

In countries where Sufi studies are full of prestige, and yet where only the 'circuses' take on almost all comers as members, there is some pressure on real Sufis to accept disciples.

TALE OF THE AMAZING EXPERIENCES

One joke about this is that of the would-be disciple who, full of what he had read in books and heard from the members of excitatory 'orders', went to talk of his experiences to a real Sufi.

'Master,' he cried, 'I have had amazing experiences of a spiritual sort, which prove to me that I am destined to become an illuminated Sufi, and you must therefore take me on as a pupil – in fact I already have students of my own!'

The Sufi smiled, and said: 'Brother, forget all this talk of "amazing experiences". The real candidates for self-realisation are those who have felt nothing at all or who do so no longer. Now what was amazing about your experiences?'

'The amazing thing is,' said the dauntless applicant, 'that these were experiences in which I experienced absolutely nothing at all...'

This is the unaltered, commanding self, in action, though such behaviour usually takes place silently, within the person, and we don't often get opportunities of seeing it externalised as beautifully as this.

Let us look at this part-conditioned, part-uncontrolled self in its various stages:

THE CONDITIONS OF THE HUMAN SELF

The Self, called the Nafs, goes through certain stages in Sufi development, first existing as a mixture of physical reactions, conditioned behaviour and various subjective aspirations.

The seven stages of the Self constitute the transformation process, ending with the stage of perfection and clarification. Some have called this process the 'refinement of the Ego'.

The stages are:

The Commanding Self
The Accusing Self
The Inspired Self
The Tranquil Self
The Satisfied Self
The Satisfying Self
The Purified and Completed Self

Each one of the words given above signifies a major characteristic of the Self in its upward ascent, hence, in Sufi eyes, most people in all cultures are generally familiar only with the first stage of the self as represented in their ethical systems as something which seeks only its own interests. The ordinary person, staying at the level of ordinary religious and moral teaching, is at the stage which the Sufis would regard as only struggling with the Commanding Self, with, in action, the Accusing Self reproaching itself for its shortcomings. It is because of this scheme that observers have styled Sufi development as going five stages beyond that known to the ordinarily 'Moral' person.

It cannot be denied that in Sufi eyes the stages of human service, for instance, and concern for others, are regarded as not very great achievements, though lauded to the skies in moralistic-centred systems as almost impossible of attainment. Hence when Saadi says in the thirteenth century:

All Adam's sons are limbs of one another,
Each of the self-same substance as his brothers,
So, while *one* member suffers ache and grief,
The other members cannot win relief.
Thou, who are heedless of thy brother's pain,
It is not right at all to name thee man...

(Gulistan, tr. Browne)

he means that the Sufis, though recognising its vital importance, still keep the door open for many stages of greater function for humankind. They maintain that to regard human well-being, though essential, as the highest possible, the sublime, achievement of humanity, is to limit oneself so much that it is, effectively, a pessimistic and unacceptably limited stance. Again, the desire for human well-being is the minimum, not the maximum, duty of humanity.

The Commanding Self is the origin of the individual controlled by a composite consciousness, which is a mixture of hopes and fears, of training and imagination, of emotional and other factors, which make up the person in his or her 'normal' state, as one would ordinarily call it. It is the state of most of the people who have not undergone the clarification process.

The Accusing Self is the state of the Self when it is able to monitor its behaviour and perceive the secondary nature of so many things formerly imagined to be primary, the actual relativity of assumed absolutes, and so on. This part of the man or woman is both the check on imperfect action and also the area through which the legitimate reproach of others or of the environment gets through to the individual. This is the stage of ordinary conscience. Most people stop and mill around here.

When the depraved or commanding self and the reproaching or accusing selves have done their work, the organ of perception and action becomes susceptible to the entry of perceptions formerly blocked. For this reason it is termed the Inspired Self. In this stage come the first indications, albeit imperfect ones, of the existence and operation of a reliable higher element, force, power or communications system.

Although people have often translated the word *Nafs*, which we call 'Self' here, as 'soul', it is in fact not such at all, but what might be called the real personality of the individual. The word for soul is '*rouh*', spirit.

The so-called lower self, the *Nafs*, passes through the stages in which it is said to 'die', and be transformed. Since it also is held to die on physical death, the phrase for this process is 'dying before you die'. Hence the death and rebirth cycle takes place in this life instead of being assigned, as in the Hindu model, to supposed literal reincarnation births and deaths.

Attempts to cause the self to operate out of sequence, that is, to receive perceptions when the third stage has not been reached, or to provoke and benefit from mystical experience before the fifth stage, produces the sort of confusion – and sometimes worse – which is reflected in some current literature of experimenters who choose their own sequence of events, and may cause developments which they cannot handle.

It also makes people crazy or nearly so. Many of these imagine themselves to be spiritual teachers, and some of them convince others that they are, too.

The inner psychological problems of people who try to force developments in their psychic life are a matter for clinical, or even experimental, psychology. But there are many who stop short of this, who have not even got to the stage where they realise that their superficial interest in metaphysics bars them from something deeper, and who try exercises mechanically or spasmodically. No wonder they try to store up with emotion.

Some of these are often otherwise quite nice people. They get superficial delusions, because of a rationalising tendency.

THE INVISIBLE TEACHER

I remember one such, whose supposed mystical career was attributed by him to 'fate' for just this kind of reason.

I lived quite near to him, and began to hear that he was passing on messages from an 'invisible teacher'.

One evening, however, he confessed to me that the teacher did not really exist.

I said: 'How could you plot such a deception? Lots of people believe you. You must be very unprincipled.'

'No,' he said. 'It is Fate. I have been chosen by a strange and mysterious method. This is how it happened.'

He had written to someone he called a 'Holy Dervish' (presumably as distinct from an unholy one) and asked him to come for a visit, to speak to a group of people in his town. He had already informed everyone he could that the great man was coming, when the appointed date arrived with no answer and no dervish. The people collected, and my friend sat on a platform before them, in silence, waiting. When everyone had been there some time, one of the local people stood up and said: 'I have understood your meaning. The Holy Dervish has not come because he is invisible and *you* are his representative. We accept you!'

'Well,' continued my friend, 'if that was not me being chosen as a teacher, through the inner working of fate, what is? I could never have *planned* such a thing!'

85

In a Sufi training system, there are rules which the members are expected to follow in that part of their development which comes within their own purview. The one which is most often quoted comes from the ancient teachings of the 'Masters of the Design', to which my own background is referred. I find that it has direct connexions with the conditions of the mind of people in both the East and West of today. Perhaps that is why the system I am about to describe is called the 'Everlasting Necessities':

THE ELEVEN RULES OF THE NAQSHBANDIYYA (MASTERS OF THE DESIGN)

Eleven mnemonic phrases refer to the framework within which the Sufic development takes place in the school often called the original teaching system of the Sufis. The Naqshbandiyya, although they have a chain of succession of mentors, believe that not all masters were public figures, but that all teachers are in inner, call it telepathic, communication.

The Naqshbandis are associated with: reviving and updating the teachings periodically; being recognised as competent to interpret all forms of Sufism; being able to initiate into all orders; using ordinary clothes and entering into the ordinary activities of the world, through which they carry on part of their work, and initiating methods which others often copy as the externals of cults.

In the psychological sense, the Eleven Rules* may be looked at in this way:

---

* The manner in which the Rules are presented will vary in accordance with the state of the student's 'self', and also with reference to the characteristics of the culture in which the teaching is projected.

1. *Awareness of Breathing.* Linked with remembering and exercise of reaching forward for subtle perceptions.
2. *Gaze on the Steps.* Awareness of actions, watchfulness of everything which one does; concentration.
3. *Travel in One's own Land.* Exploration of the student's own mind by himself, establishing the watchfulness connected with the transformation of the Self.
4. *Solitude in Company.* The ability to remove one's consciousness from company, as well as to re-attach it.
5. *Remembering.* Conceiving that there is an 'interrupted' contact between humanity and the beyond. The posture of reaching mentally to it helps to restore the contact; dedication.
6. *Restraint.* Literally, 'pulling back', a technical term for prayer in a certain form.
7. *Watchfulness.* The exclusion of distractions, and alertness for subtle perceptions.
8. *Recollection.* Also termed 'noting', this stands for becoming aware of Absolute Truth as in some sense present.
9. *Pause of Time.* Reprise of thought and action, and other pauses in time.
10. *Pause of Numbers.* Awareness of the number of repetitions of a certain formula; certain forms of counting.
11. *Pause of the Heart.* Visualisation of the heart; special exercise of an identification of the individual with the ultimate.

The way in which these exercises are carried out is a matter for personal tuition. The teacher monitors and prescribes for alterations in awareness which follow these practices. They are subject to careful adjustment and cannot be automatically performed.

Certain special movements and visualisations, combined
with other factors, are employed in various schemes of the
Sufis to help to develop subtler stages of consciousness.

Luckily, most people who involve themselves in imitations
of these studies on their own initiative stay at the stage where
they do little harm to themselves or to others. It is, in fact,
far better that they should play at being mystics than that
they should become obsessional or fall into the hands of
charlatans.

* * *

BEARD, CLOAK AND ROSARY

I cannot resist, thinking of ancient formulae, referring to
the story of the man with a bushy beard, wearing a rosary
around his neck, dressed in a hooded cloak, with long and
greasy hair, who was anxious, recently, to tell everyone that
he was 'A Sufi'.

Someone – who really *was* a Sufi – asked him why he was
behaving like that. He said: 'I am following the instructions
and information contained in this ancient handbook for
disciples.'

'But,' said the real Sufi, 'that cannot apply now – it was
written several centuries ago…'

'That may well be,' said the new 'Sufi', 'but *I* only found it
last month!'

* * *

The schemata just given will indicate that the Sufi approach
is characterised by a systematic dealing with a succession
of developments in the learner, to avoid distorted results.

Many of the supposedly magical and mystical procedures which are found in books, ascribed to other teachings, have been recognised by Sufis and others as having been based on a partial understanding of these processes, or ones similar to them. This may reinforce the Sufi assertion that there is essentially only one method of carrying on these investigations, and that that method – prominent features of which I am now citing – itself emerges from the insight obtained from penetrating beyond normal limitations. It is, in short, the original framework of what has been called the 'science of man', certainly for centuries before the phrase became current as 'the human sciences'.

As a recent example of this assessment, made by someone looking at Sufi ideas and practices objectively (in the sense that he is not an occultist, orientalist or Sufi) we can observe the view of the well-known poet Ted Hughes, who wrote – after a consideration of the published materials:

> One often comes across references to the 'secret doctrine', some mysterious brotherhood that is said to hold the keys to everything in the West outside Christianity, that touches the occult: tarot cards...secret societies, Rosicrucians, Masons, The Kabbalah. [It is now clear] that in fact all these things originated among the Sufis and represent degenerate, strayed filterings of the doctrine...[thus] many forlorn puzzles in the world...suddenly come into organic life...*

Two points are worth making here. First, most of the external formulations referred to by Hughes, and many

---

* Ted Hughes, in *The Listener* (London) October 29, 1964.

more, have been traced to temporary teaching groups in the Middle East by scholars and others, and the materials have been in print for a good number of years. The Sufis do not claim to have originated all of them, but they traditionally *have* claimed that, at the point of higher consciousness attained to by various mystical formulations, the Sufi experience and that of such 'other' frameworks is identical. There is very little doubt, either, that this kind of grouping is to be found at the present time, in general, only in a very defective and overgrown form, as mere cults. Second, the reference to Christianity is rather wide of the mark, for the Sufi understanding of Christianity is so deep that Sufis are often called 'secret Christians' in the East, and esteem Jesus as a Teacher of the Path, combining the instrumental and prophetic functions. As already noted, Sufis were regarded as authorities on Christianity in the Middle Ages in the Christian West. They believe, however, that dogma and liturgy are bases, not ultimates, and that direct experience of religion is the objective of which externals are stepping-stones. The cargo-cult was in operation in the West long before the New Guinea people discovered it...

As we continue with our consideration of Sufi theoretical and practical approaches to inner knowledge, we will be able to note two things which are of present-day interest. The first is that the setting up of a group of concepts, to enable the mind to approach something, can easily become, in insensitive hands, stabilised as a cult. Second, that, in approaching the cultivation of deeper awareness, the Sufis have postulated and employed sequences of experiences based on the ever-deeper and successively superseded ranges of understanding. In most more familiar systems we have, on the contrary, only one form of 'higher consciousness': for the Sufis there are at least five.

THE FIVE SUBTLETIES

This brings us to the conceptual framework of the Five Subtleties. The human being is stated, in Sufi presentation, to contain five elements of the 'relative' and five of the 'absolute'. Five, that is, which belong to secondary things, referred to as The World, and five which are beyond limitation or dimensions, and which refer to the different manifestations of the various levels of consciousness beyond ordinarily recognisable physics.

There are said to be five centres of spiritual perception, corresponding to these ranges of experience. They are conceived of as having physical locations in the human body.

These Five Subtleties (*Lataif-i-Khamsa*) do not exist literally. They are located in the body because the postures of extending attention to these areas are held to orientate the mind towards higher understanding and illumination.

The secondary, or 'Commanding' self – which rules the personality most of the time and which provides the barrier against extradimensional perception – is not one of these Subtle organs, but it has a 'location', in the area of the navel. Concentration on this spot may be said to be connected with the attempt to transform this Self.

But we are dealing with the higher faculties. They are named as follows:

MIND, on the left side, whose 'field' is
   approximately where the heart is. Called QALB
   = the Heart centre;
SPIRIT, on the right side, opposite MIND. This is
   known as ROUH, sometimes translated as the
   Soul centre;

SECRET, the first stage of higher consciousness, located between the first two, in the solar plexus. The original term is SIRR, which has been called 'inner consciousness';

MYSTERIOUS, in the forehead between the eyes but just above them. Its name is KHAFI, which carries the connotation of deep secrecy;

and finally comes

THE DEEPLY HIDDEN, which is resident in the brain and whose 'field' of operation may move between the brain and the centre of the chest. Its technical name is AKHFA, which stands for 'most hidden'.

The organ of stimulation of the Five Centres is the transformed consciousness, the personality originally found in the form of the Commanding Self, when it has been through its refining process.

The concentration upon certain colours helps to awaken them: MIND is equated with yellow; SPIRIT with red; SECRET (consciousness) with white; MYSTERIOUS with black and DEEPLY HIDDEN with green.

We must always remember that this is descriptive, and that the student has to go through with the experience of it. It is not enough to memorise, as many people do, this kind of material, and imagine that one knows something. It is harmful to experiment with these centres.

This imagining that one has knowledge because one has a description of an instrument is common in all cultures. It is well known in the teaching of Western-type knowledge in the East, where people may take your word for things you want them to work through.

WHAT THE TEACHER KNOWS

In a story about this, one Eastern student said to another:
'I don't think that our new American geometry teacher knows much.'
'How come?' asks his friend.
'Well, he said "The square on the hypotenuse of a right-angled triangle is equal to the sum of the squares on the other two sides", and I said "Yes". But he couldn't have been very sure of his facts, for he then said: "Now YOU prove it!"'

Just as there are several forms of consciousness, which have to be awakened and experienced, to avoid distortions or failure, in a certain manner, carefully researched, there are four types of so-called miraculous happenings. Again, the Sufis – unlike other extant schools – do not merely seek wonders or label them all as significant. They work with them in accordance with certain scales of value.

WONDERS AND MIRACLES

First of these are those appearances which are due to works of deception, such as conjurors use, works of stealth, technically termed *Istidraj*, 'successive things'.

Second come amazing things done by people without their knowing exactly how they do them, through the help of certain entities and influences. These works are called *Ma'awanat*, 'aids'. This is the lowest form of activities which appear to violate the natural order. Concentration on these things prevents higher human development. The energy going into them cannot be focussed properly, and the enterprise usually degenerates into charlatanry or remains a hit-or-miss occultism.

Third we have wonder-working (*Karāmāt*), which literally means something generously bestowed. These are apparent variations in physical laws (actually using unfamiliar ones), carried out in the course of the Sufi's role as someone endowed with special functions. This ability evaporates if not employed operationally. Operationally means: 'only in accordance with the harmony of the entire Sufi phenomenon'.

Fourth, and finally, are what are termed *real* miracles – the word for them is *Mu'ajizāt*. These are true violations of natural events, carried out before witnesses by deliberate intent, by prophets, who are further defined as lawgivers. The purpose is evidentiary, as in the case of the miracles in the Old and New Testaments.

The three kinds of operation correspond to the degree of significance and role of the human agent in question. Sleight of hand, of course, is for performers and charlatans. Assistances come to worthy people, but carry with them the probability that such undeveloped individuals will ascribe them to wild and unlikely sources. There are considerable risks of self-deception in pursuing this kind of thing. Sufi wonder-working comes about to help the Sufi in his work. It is his duty, in general, to conceal these happenings; and it is traditional also that his fellow-workers and disciples should also conceal them, if they know about their ever having happened.

Miracles as such only take place when there is a need to demonstrate a person's importance before a mass of people, or a variety of people of all kinds, so that they will listen to the message which he has for them relating to religious organisation. They have never been, and are not now any part of Sufic activity.

A FLOWERLESS GARDEN

These schemata, as I have said, part of an ongoing and complete tradition, are of little value simply on the printed page, and even less when merely adopted without the technical knowledge and total situation necessary. But to record them and display some part of the pattern is just about worthwhile. It certainly shows how other systems look like partial derivations from these very schemata. But looked at *without activity* one can say of them something like that man said when he was shown a certain garden: 'Take away the flowers and design, and what have you got, after all?'

When there is a Sufi school, it has its own pace of travelling, and its carefully balanced character must be preserved. People always want more for less, always seek stimulation from materials and hardly ever think of the enormous amount of work which lies behind many a successful human (and every single spiritual) operation.

GOING FASTER...

I often think about a certain story, when I remember that the Sufi activity must remain coherent in the sense of being one whole, which you cannot desert, or simplify, without dismantling it. This is why, however much you might like an easier ride with this subject, I can't give it to you. This story is about the man in a slow train which had stopped, for the hundredth time, at a wayside station. He jumped out of his carriage and ran to the driver. 'Can't you go any faster?' he roared at him.

'Yes, sir, I can certainly go faster – but I am not allowed to leave the train!'

IV   The Teaching Story – 1

People who speak little need only half a brain
— Italian proverb

I CAN THINK of no better way of beginning a consideration of stories than with a very short, true story, about the situation, the real intricacies, of dealing not only with stories, but with the talking and hearing process itself.

I was giving a lecture recently on the difficulty which people have in taking things in, especially at any speed, even if they do it sequentially; and how a story, or even a statement, might become a person's possession, as it were, so that it could be recalled to mind and considered from various points of view. 'It has been noticed,' I continued, 'that much information is *not* absorbed because many people cannot really absorb something when they have heard it only once...'

Immediately a hand went up, and someone sitting in the front row asked me: 'Would you mind saying that again?' I later enquired, and found out that he was neither hard of hearing nor a quick-witted humorist.

This time-lag, between the presentation of materials and their integration into the thinking and repertoire of action of the individual, has itself to be taught, we find, to quite a lot of people interested in stories. It is useful to other people, too, but we find it easy to observe and to test in the story-telling and story-hearing atmosphere. The holistic mode will obtain certain parts, and the more literal others. Neither will perceive many dimensions until a skill has been developed. This short Sufi tale is employed for the educational purpose of establishing in the mind the contention at least that one may need this time-lapse for this purpose, and it is not intended to make fun of any of the fictional figures appearing in it:

TIME AND POMEGRANATES

A disciple went to the house of a Sufi physician and asked to become an apprentice in the art of medicine.

'You are impatient,' said the doctor, 'and so you will fail to observe things which you will need to learn.'

But the young man pleaded, and the Sufi agreed to accept him.

After some years the youth felt that he could exercise some of the skills which he had learnt. One day a man was walking towards the house and the doctor – looking at him from a distance – said: 'That man is ill. He needs pomegranates.'

'You have made the diagnosis – let *me* prescribe for him, and I will have done half the work,' said the student.

'Very well,' said the teacher, 'providing that you remember that action should also be looked at as illustration.'

As soon as the patient arrived at the doorstep, the student brought him in and said: 'You are ill. Take pomegranates.'

'Pomegranates!' shouted the patient, 'pomegranates to you – nonsense!' And he went away.

The young man asked his master what the meaning of the interchange had been.

'I will illustrate it the next time we get a similar case,' said the Sufi.

Shortly afterwards the two were sitting outside the house when the master looked up briefly and saw a man approaching.

'Here is an illustration for you – a man who needs pomegranates,' he said.

The patient was brought in, and the doctor said to him:

'You are a difficult and intricate case, I can see that. Let me see…yes, you need a special diet. This must be composed of something round, with small sacs inside it, naturally occurring. An orange…that would be of the wrong colour…lemons are too acidic…I have it: pomegranates!'

The patient went away, delighted and grateful.

'But Master,' said the student, 'why did you not say "pomegranates" straight away?'

'Because,' said the Sufi, 'he needed *time* as well as pomegranates.'*

Now, this tale usually produces some laughter, but sometimes, especially in cultures where people have acquired the habit of turning as many things as possible into wisecracks, we occasionally get such comments as 'that patient was a real idiot, wasn't he?'

ABOLITION OF IMPACT

The abolition of the impact of a story or other stimulus is, of course, well known as a device, a way of avoiding the assimilation of its point, and this behaviour can frequently be seen in people who have the need, displayed, too, in other ways, of protecting themselves against outside influences. Other tales are used as a corrective to this, enabling people to laugh at themselves or to recognise that there is no *sin* in being prone to the same deficiencies as very many other people are.

---

* Idries Shah, *The Dermis Probe*, London: Jonathan Cape, 1970, p. 72f.

I have come across very few reactions as dramatic as the one which followed my first publication, in 1969, of an ancient narrative *about* dramatic reactions. In something like 1500 words, well spaced out and occupying nine pages with plenty of white space, I retold the legend of the man who had a very big book with only a few words written in it, the words being concerned with how people judged by appearances and confused the container with the content, as it were, and were enraged when they found that this book has so few words in it. These nine pages were printed and published as a book, with some 300 other – blank – pages to bulk it out. The external shape, size and weight of this volume, which I entitled *The Book of The Book*,* presumably gave the impression that it had words right the way through, was filled with words. And the cover was gold-embossed.

There was an immediate outcry. Reviewers, seeing that it had only nine pages of print, manifested their rage and disappointment at such a product. None of them, at first, noticed that it was a book about people who were seized by rage and disappointment when a book turned out to have nothing in it except something about people who were annoyed when they found that a book only warned about the container and the content. Presently, however, one by one, other reviewers started to see the point and to give it *good* reviews. It has now run through four editions: but not before an expert at the British Museum in London unhesitatingly declared that it was 'not a book at all', until we found a book which proved that it really did fulfil the criteria of a book laid down by UNESCO...Now and again I see references to it as

---

* Idries Shah: *The Book of the Book*, London 1969, 70, 73, 76.

'causing a sensation' or as 'experimental and new', even in the London *Times*.

The confusion of the container and the content, of course, is a very common human tendency, causing the worship of externals and producing magic-wand type thinking, but for some reason called cargo-cultism only when it is found among under-developed peoples...The argument and illustration that there are these two modes – the inner and the outer shape – by means of stories such as this, makes it possible for the student to recall and replay, as it were, the model story and then to study his own behaviour to see whether, perhaps, he is developing a tendency towards superficiality, magical thinking or incomplete attention.

ANALOGICAL TEACHING

Sufi analogical teaching has an interesting dimension which, as one becomes more familiar with it, can be observed almost everywhere. This is summed up in the statement that 'things which have a mental form also have a physical one: and also a form reflected in social happenings'. If the container is the human being, the content may be called the nature and quality of his inner self; whether you call this psychological, educational or spiritual. Sometimes you can see the literal disparity between container and content displayed, almost as a moral lesson or even as a social drama, in real life. This is what gives teaching-stories their reality, and also endows teaching narratives (accounts of contacts between teachers and learners) their vitality.

Here is an example of how the human neglectfulness of container and content in the inner sense can actually concretise itself in a real-life occurrence:

Last year the London *Times* reported* that one local authority in a British county had received a parcel on which they had to pay a heavy excess postage charge, since it bore no stamp. It was so badly packed that it had burst open in transit. Inside this interesting package, this container with such a disastrously negligent outwardness, what do you think there was? Nothing less than 200 leaflets from the Post Office Users' Council. They were entitled: 'Have you a complaint about the Post Office?'

Here is another one, picked almost at random, which raises even deeper questions about container and content:

NUTRITION FROM THE CONTAINER

Four years ago it was stated that scientific tests had been carried out on the characteristics of various breakfast cereals and their containers. Rats were fed, in laboratory conditions, on diets of both the contents and the containers. The results indicate, and I quote, 'that the box cardboard is often more nutritious than the cereals inside'.**

I would draw a lesson from these instances to warn against assumptions about what one puts in, in imagined Sufi study, and what is really there, let alone what one puts it into.

When people have in fact become attached to externals, stories, often jokes, can be used to enable them to acquire a more constructive perspective. In Sufi circles it is not uncommon for a Sufi to prevent attachment to himself from the students, and to draw attention to the total phenomenon of the Sufi enterprise instead. We can take such a story as

* *The Times*, London, 24 December 1975, p. 2, col. 6.
** *The Observer* (magazine section), London, 31 March 1974, p. 41, col. 1.

this one to impart the 'shock' which takes concentration *off* superficialities or irrelevancies, so that it may attach itself to something more fundamental, if less palpable:

'INNERMOST' FEELINGS

Now here is a Western story, but it will serve for this purpose. There was once a man who travelled to a far distant land to seek spiritual enlightenment. Finally he arrived at the dwelling of a sage who was reputed to be a master of secrets. At the precise moment that he was ushered into the presence of the great one, a strange agitation seized him, and he fell to the ground, feeling that the very earth might open up and swallow him.

'At last – at last,' he stammered, 'you have stirred my innermost being, Master of spiritual exaltation…'

'I am afraid I do not quite understand,' said the venerable teacher, 'how you can imagine that you can benefit from what was, in fact, only an earthquake. We have a lot of them around here, you know…'

It should be remembered that Sufi educational technique aims at removing, or helping to remove, superficial behaviour-pattern barriers to deeper understanding. This is because the concept of the exclusion of limiting factors is every bit as important among the Sufis as the inclusion of concepts and the use of special techniques for stimulating perceptions: indeed, the former must precede the latter.

Because most people will tend to adopt the outer practices of people and institutions which they respect or admire, many Sufi tales provide humorous or semi-humorous formats which can be recalled to mind to reduce this incrustation's effect in such cases. Most of the Sufi and other spiritual schools publicly known, whether here or elsewhere, are *visibly*, and for the Sufi effectively, disabled in their learning potential by exactly this accretion problem.

There is a tale which covers this; though it, like many other Sufi stories, also carries other dimensions which come to light when the consciousness is able to deal with them.

STEALING ADVICE

A man once applied to a Sufi to become his disciple, but was rejected, as not being ready for this path. So he decided that he would learn what he could by direct methods. What could be wrong in adopting Sufi practice?

Finding out that a new disciple was being enrolled that evening, he climbed onto the roof of the Sufi meeting-place and listened to the first instructions being given by the Teacher:

'Do not walk on the left-hand side of a street; do not avoid a fortunate person; do not push yourself forward before others.' Well, that seemed easy enough to the eavesdropper, who, naturally, at once proceeded to apply these teachings to his own life.

But, as he was walking home along the right-hand side of a street, a plant-pot fell on him from a balcony, and he was injured. Making friends with a prosperous merchant, all that happened was that the man swindled him. Finally, when he tried to apply for employment to feed himself (as he had lost all his money) he found that there were always other applicants there first, and without pushing he was unable even to obtain an interview.

Now, the tale continues, *did* he realise that the instructions were scripted, prescribed *only* for the man whom the Sufi had been talking to? Certainly not; he concluded that the

Sufi was a fraud, even an agent of the Devil. And, of course, it was because he was not yet ready for calculated, measured instructions that the Sufi had rejected his candidature in the first place.

These story-structures, in addition to displaying common features of human action, have two major functions. The first is to provide indications of the barriers to learning; the second is to place in the hands of the student the means to administer, to some degree, self-correction through feedback. These tales are used instead of community disciplines because Sufis do not organise into monastic or other 'orders' in which people are conditioned. The reason for this, of course, is that Sufis hold that such training may become another form of straitjacket, and tends to produce automatism and conditioned response behaviour, removing the element of choice in thought and action which is only available when the alternatives are known and the conditioning does not impose a certain so-called choice. The Sufi 'orders' known to history are late elaborations of the externals of schools.

(Although many of these so-called orders are named after their putative founders, they are later developments. Even historical research concurs in general with authentic contemporary Sufi teaching that there is neither proof nor reason for great teachers of the past actually organising such restrictive institutions. Indeed, it would make nonsense of much of their teaching if they did.)

Like any other instruments, Sufi tales can be *misused*, and when – as is not infrequently true – both the supposed teacher (who tries to apply the stories from, say, books and is not himself a product of them) and the would-be learner are *not* operating within the real Sufi frame, nothing useful will happen at all. Unless you call propaganda or emotional stimulus useful: and you can get those anywhere.

THE SYMPTOMS

The following passage indicates one side of the situation which then obtains.

Someone asked a wise man, 'I have heard that humanity is suffering from an ailment which prevents men and women from seeing truth, from knowing themselves. What is the main symptom?'

He answered: 'The first symptom is to believe that one is *not* suffering from this illness at all. But when it *really* starts to take hold, the patient may *agree* that he is ill, but now insists that the disease is anything other than actually it is.'

This disordered perception is very marked in heroic but ill-considered attempts at obtaining esoteric knowledge, which really means 'simultaneous' knowledge, all over the world today.

Sufi teaching takes place within a system which is much more often than not indirect. It is sometimes unperceived at the moment of its operation, though not always in its externals. The thirteenth-century teacher Jalaluddin Rumi refers to this indirect operational quality of stories which one often observes in action, through an actual tale – a tale explaining how a tale can work:

There was once a merchant who kept a parrot imprisoned in a cage. When about to visit India, on a business trip, he said to the bird:

'I am travelling to your homeland. Can I give any message to your relatives there?'

'Simply tell them,' said the parrot, 'that I am living here in a cage.'

When the merchant returned, he said to the parrot:

'I am sorry to have to tell you that when I found and informed your wild relatives in the jungle that you were caged, the shock was too much for one of them. As soon as he heard the news, he dropped from his branch, no doubt having died from grief.'

Immediately he had spoken, the parrot collapsed and lay inert on the floor of his cage.

Sorrowfully, the merchant took him and placed him outside in the garden. Then the parrot, having got the message, sat up and flew away, out of reach.

We must not think either that this exhausts the symbolism of this story, or that it will necessarily appeal to everyone. Rumi himself once said that counterfeit gold is only to be found because there is such a thing as *real* gold to be copied. And there is a true story, of something which took place in Britain not so long ago, which verifies our experience that many of our stories (and especially the events in them) appear on the surface to be so trivial to so many people that they reject them completely.

A jeweller in Birkenhead, Cheshire, in England, wanted to get people into his shop.* He handed out 3,000 stones to people in the street. They all looked like real diamonds, but all but four of them were glass. He explained, in a leaflet given to each recipient, that there were real diamonds among the give-away stones. Whoever got a stone of any kind was invited to visit the jewellery store, to find out if they had been lucky. Out of the 3,000 people getting the stones, only one – a woman – actually turned up at the shop. She was right: she had a genuine diamond. All the rest of the people, presumably, thought that they were *all* fakes. The real diamonds had been as quickly discarded as the spurious.

Now, if this kind of thing can happen with things as concrete as stones, and if people are in general as neglectful of possibilities as to provide only one individual in three

---

*   *Daily Mail*: 'Giveaway Diamonds', by Tom Hendry, 20 July 1972, p. 3, col. 5.

thousand to have hope for success, you can see an instant analogy with our own experience.

The analogy includes the minus factors that people can call us fakes for peddling silly old stories and refuse to seek further. It also carries with it, however, the plus that enough people think that we are harmless peddlers of old stories to allow us to continue on our way...

Both the Qur'an in the seventh century and the writings of Rumi in the thirteenth (and many other books) have been opposed by wiseacres, and the 'wise', on exactly the grounds that they were just 'filled with old fables', which could not possibly be of any use to anyone. So we remain in respectable company.

But even fables, stories of less deep outer messages than that of indirect teaching, can be used, and are widely used, to accustom even quite small children to the future realities of life in the Middle East and Central Asia, the heartland of my basic culture.

But you do not have to be a child to accept or to reject stories as vehicles for psychological action or knowledge...

When someone asked me on BBC Radio once why I used so many of other people's tales and did not make up any of my own, I said that nobody had asked me for my own. So the interviewer, of course, immediately asked me to tell an original one, which I did. A friend of mine had the radio on in his office at the time and asked his secretary what she thought of it. She said: 'No wonder nobody ever asks him – his stories are terrible...' But the main reason to adopt traditional tales is, of course, that you don't try to manufacture your own instrument if you already have a range of them, superbly made and totally effective, fashioned by master craftsmen.

From the Sufi understanding of human thinking, of course, the secretary could hardly be expected to rave about a story if she had other priorities on her mind. It is never easy to get publishers, for instance, to publish collections of Sufi tales if they first see the manuscript and judge that they are of what they call 'uneven quality'. Judging the tales for punch, humour, interest or whether they say anything to you at a given moment is using the stories in a way in which they are not intended to be used. An instrument is useful or not, according to whether circumstances are correct.

THE CAMELMAN AND THE PLASTIC

There is a true tale about this. I once showed a piece of clear plastic to a camelman. He looked at it and said: 'Interesting, but there is no future in it.'

I asked him why.

'Well,' he said, 'it is not sufficiently transparent to see through properly, it is probably very costly, you can't wear it, and it would not keep the glare out if I used it for a window in a tent...'

One great advantage of Sufi tales and narratives of encounters which I see – but which many others find irksome – is that they help to make real to the mind the fact that everything has its own, correct time. Now, this is a part of our daily experience (you cannot catch a train if it is not there, for instance, apart from all the other prerequisites needed to get on that train) but people tend to imagine that this sort of argument is always advanced to *stop* someone doing something, or to avoid having to do it. It is Sufi experience that people who can keep calm enough to realise that there might be a time and a place – and other requirements – for anything, are *more*, not less, able to benefit from that thing.

Here is a story which is almost always taken to mean that certain things are impossible, but which need not mean that at all:

FISH OUT OF WATER

A would-be disciple begged a Sufi master to teach him exercises. The Sufi, however, said: 'I am going to tell you a *story* instead – then you won't *need* exercises.' He continued: 'There was once a man who agreed to train a fish who begged him to help, to live out of the water; being desperate to take up a life on land. Little by little, a few seconds and then a few minutes, then hours at a time, he managed to get it accustomed to the open air. In fact the fish went to live near him, with its own damp but open-air place in a flower-bed in the man's garden. It was delighted with its new life, and often used to say to him: "This is what I call real *living*!" Then, one day, there was a very heavy downpour of rain, which flooded the garden – and the fish was drowned.'

It makes a good laugh, and it can sound like a derisive tale. But the story only refers to *fish*, and as it is a story, 'fish' does not have to be an unalterable condition of the person being told it...

The usefulness of the teaching-story is boundless under the right conditions, though severely limited under two circumstances: the first of these, of course, is when people think of stories as trivial and only belonging to entertainment or for the inculcation of morals, and so on, as in the current versions of the fables of Aesop. Even if they are seen to show up amusing sides of human nature, this usage, this opinion about them, blunts their impact. So we can never be confident about their opportuneness until some context has been given about the traditional importance of the story, to enable our hearers to re-acquire flexibility of mental approach. The other limiting circumstance is when people have for some reason become so bemused by an attitude of awe and a desire for amazing secrets that they are, effectively, consuming that experience, the experience of awe, and get 'turned on', amazed and bemused by the story itself.

It is generally felt that these two attitudes are linked with the individual's desire to define exactly what the story phenomenon is, ahead of his willingness to have explained to him that it is a subtle and very sophisticated instrument. Such attitudes, incidentally, may betray the underlying motivation of the individual concerned as being a thirst for either order or excitement. Is it, we may ask, a desire for knowledge or self-development? We seldom find it wise to dissolve this 'fixation of choice', as it might be called, since the result usually is someone who may not now be fixated on an erroneous expectation from stories: but still has the desire for, say, explanations or emotional stimulus. The production of basic psychological balance is not the main job of the Sufi, who is always, moreover, aware of the significance of the saying: 'Before killing the cat, make arrangements about the mice.'

Teaching-stories *do* serve as correctives for various psychological conditions, though they are not primarily employed as a therapy, but rather as an illustration of what people are really like. The therapeutic effect, if any, would take place as a part of the entire operation of involvement in the tradition. This is seen as a harmonisation, and not a treatment. The symptoms disappear, that is to say, when the ailment is not commanding a portion of the student's attention, which is extended for other purposes. The aim to provide the attention-capacity with fruitful objects of attention does not treat the symptoms, and does not treat the disease. The disease ceases to exist when the whole being is harmoniously balanced. It is not regarded as a therapeutic process, because the intention is not to cure and the procedures are not aimed at the ailment or to make the person feel better, or even to operate better on the ordinary psychological plane.

The restoration of the harmony of the individual has, it is believed, higher aims than that, of which a *by-product* should be the vanishing of the disability.

When a *real* interest takes over, psychological troubles are remarkably often exorcised by it: a sort of reverse of the proverb: 'When the house catches fire, the toothache flies out of the window.'

This is more than a theory, seen from the Sufi perspective; for the learning-system, including the use of stories, is both primary and also the same element as has produced the Sufi exponent himself: the teaching is hence not exterior to the practice; and our kind of study is therefore participation activity. It is not objective in the sense that we can have, say, gardeners who never touch a plant, or experts on government who teach it but have never been near a government, let alone having discharged any functions connected therewith.

The motivation to study Sufism, or even to familiarise oneself with any of the system's procedures, will, according to the Sufis, only yield results to the extent to which the field as a whole has truly been entered into. Students-at-a-distance will always, of course, continue to obtain what they can from this and all other kinds of study. But the bits and pieces which can be obtained by this method will probably be produced by many other methods, including much more 'respectable' scientific ones, given enough time. There is a short tale which emphasises the value of knowing what one is aiming for:

WHAT HE WAS TRYING TO DO

A man went to a Sufi and said:

'My neighbour makes my life a misery by visiting me at all hours, hanging about the house and constantly asking questions.'

The Sufi advised:

'Nothing is easier than the cure for this. All you have to do is to ask the man for money every time you see him, and he will soon start to avoid you.'

'But supposing he then goes about the town telling everyone that I am a beggar?'

'Ah,' said the wise man, 'I see that you are hoping to control the thoughts of mankind, not trying to stop your neighbour annoying you. Do you *often* imagine that you want one thing when you really want another?'

The Sufi teaching-story, above all, does not require anyone to dress in comic clothes and adopt a peculiar attitude towards anyone or anything. It expects people to enlarge their horizons, but it has to have its own requirements fulfilled in order to operate to an appropriate degree. The introduction of this material into the West attracts all kinds of expectations, and some of them will undoubtedly produce hybrid results which could be absurd. Like all other forms of learning, it needs its own basic teaching institution – and that is not a do-it-yourself one. Someone engaged in self-study, runs the proverb, should not have a fool for a teacher. One story which is current in the West can be used to illustrate what I mean:

DOING YOUR OWN THING

A man once crossed a carrier pigeon with a parrot, so that its offspring could speak its message instead of having to carry a written one. But the bird which was produced by this experiment took hours instead of minutes to finish its journey.

'Why did you take so long?' the man asked it.

'Well, it was such a beautiful day,' said the superior bird, 'that I walked.' This is why you have Aesop and wise saws instead of developmental instruments: you choose the inculcation of morals alone, or mainly so.

One can't help thinking of this story today, when people mix all sorts of techniques and exercises in trying for spiritual realisation. Their results are as mixed up as the bird in the fable. The results of such hybridising experiments can be long-lasting. Many are to be found in the East, and persist as circuses whose participants, generally, dislike stories and really do fear humour. They call themselves 'spiritual', however.

And, since we are talking about tales from the East, we can invoke a slightly different angle on the same subject: that this is an intact tradition with its own requirements. The stories belong to a whole spectrum of reality, they do not mix with cults and bits and pieces. Rather roughly, for the sensibilities of some of the delightful people who are perhaps accustomed to gentler treatment, I take the liberty of quoting a traditional saying often used by people less polished than you or I: 'If you have been asleep in a kennel, do not ask why you get up in the morning covered with fleas...'

It is important, at the very least, to familiarise oneself with the whole available range of stories put out in this manner, for they are to be considered the facets of a whole. And in addition, the individual story must be given close attention, so that it can yield its optimum value. To go from one to another choosing those which appeal, and giving no attention to those which do not stimulate us so much, however human a reaction, is a sign of a bad and unpromising student in this field. Our habits of lingering over the more desired or more pleasing things in life, when carried over into serious study can sometimes be barriers to progress in understanding. The difference between these two approaches was borne upon me one day recently in an entirely different connection.

WHY DIDN'T YOU SAY?

I was staying in the palace of a Middle Eastern potentate not very long ago, surrounded by every luxury. In the morning the major-domo arrived to take any orders, and I thought I would like to hear the radio: but there was not one in my apartments.

I asked him to arrange it. 'I would like to listen to the radio, please.'

'Of course. What programme?'

'The early-morning BBC World Service news.'

The following morning two men arrived, bearing the most advanced radio receiver I had ever seen. 'Where would you like it set up?'

'Right over here will do fine.'

One man sited the set, the other put on headphones and located the station. He looked at his watch. Very soon he gave a signal, and the radio amplifier was switched on. At full loudspeaker volume I heard the stirring march tune identifying London, Lillibulero…Then the news. When it was over, the two picked up their apparatus, and silently withdrew.

After breakfast, I went to pay my respects to the potentate, who asked me if all was to my liking.

'Yes, may your life be long! I did ask them to give me the London news, and they did, but I wish they had left the radio, so that I could listen to other programmes…'

'My dear fellow,' said the sovereign, for he had been educated in England and spoke like that, 'you must not blame us, but rather the fact that you are spending a little too much time in the West. Why *on earth* didn't you tell my chaps that you only wanted to twiddle? *Then* they would have left it…'

SO, IF PEOPLE INTERESTED IN EASTERN TALES ONLY WANT TO TWIDDLE, THEY SHOULD *SAY SO*…

They can, on the other hand, look at the intact system, whether presented as Eastern or as a psychological and educational tool.

Having insisted that access to the whole range of the activity of Sufi study can only come through involvement in it, as with any other comprehensive operation, one can certainly enunciate other principles which may be of interest and of use to more generalised human areas: though I must stress that they are limited.

The zoologist Dr Desmond Morris (who wrote *The Naked Ape* and other best-selling books on human behaviour) has noted the effect of Sufi stories on his daily life. Many of these, he states, were not appreciated by him at the time of reading, but their message and usefulness were understood when, subsequently, experiences corresponding to the structures laid down in the stories occurred in his dealings with other people. There was a *framework* for handling situations which he had not had before.

THE TALES AS STRUCTURES

Several scholars, both those specialising in the Middle East and others, have written recently that the tales – as *structures* which make possible the holding of certain concepts in a particular relationship – have an *unusual* value, sometimes in helping them to understand ranges of ideas which are not ordinarily linked in any other way. And, in the scientific field, for instance, the Mulla Nasrudin stories appear in, of all things, the Report of the Second Coral Gables Conference on Symmetry Principles at High Energy, to illustrate recondite concepts in physics. An interesting experiment is now going on showing that the usage of unfamiliar and even confusing stories and statements could be rendered in terms of one method of switching the brain's action from the sequential and logical to the simultaneous mode.

In this latter area, several Sufi tales in my *Tales of the Dervishes* * which have no obvious 'point' or which are susceptible to more than one interpretation, have been observed to work in this way. The bringing into greater action of the right-hemisphere functions and the attenuation of the left, may well be the reason for such disjointed injunctions as 'Think of the sound of no sound'.

I have myself been impressed to hear a small schoolboy, faced by the flow of words of an unusually lucid and logical youth, shout suddenly at him, 'Go knit yourself a slice of cake!' The effect was almost instantaneous, stopping the intellectual in his tracks. But it is hardly fair to use this knowledge deliberately to overcome someone else.

The holistic overall mode cannot of course compete in sequential activity, and seems to take over when the logical one is jammed by such statements as this. I once did this as a test when a Freudian psychiatrist was holding forth on something or other in highly respectful company, lucidly and persuasively. I said: 'Well, all Freudians are always saying things like "we must find out whether his grandmother bit him in the womb..."' The poor man gasped and stammered, and all he could say was, rather weakly, 'But it is physically impossible for that to happen', and this drew such a roar of derision from the audience, whose brains were evidently sequentially operating, that he never regained his aplomb in their company.

---

* Idries Shah: *Tales of the Dervishes*, London 1967, etc., New York 1969, etc.

THE SECRET PROTECTING ITSELF

The more recognisably 'Eastern mystical master' type of tale has an undeniable value in placing relationships into a new perspective, providing that it is employed within limits. If, for instance, these tales are read only as didactic and propagandist, designed to instil belief and create submission to the 'master's' wisdom, they cannot be used for *our* teaching purposes; consequently they get fed into indoctrination cults, or something which has turned or will turn into such a cult. If the message (that there are certain times and circumstances, certain arrangements of factors, which have to be observed in order to learn the things being taught by the tradition) is respected and not confused with one-upmanship, the tales can be extremely valuable. I sometimes ask myself, though, whether the phrase much used by Sufis, 'The secret protects itself', cannot be applied to such tales, as well as to other areas in Sufi experience – for a paranoid reaction to them effectively excludes the paranoid from that which they have to convey. Such stories are not, of course, the ingenuous attempts by crude esotericists from the East to impress and intimidate enquirers, or to bend them to their will: though some could be used for this by such people. Many an instrument can be used for cruder purposes than its original function. Indeed, one purpose of this exposition of mine is to put people on their guard.

Let us look at a sample of this kind of tale, with its built-in aversion-therapy element, likely to annoy and deflect anyone who thinks only that he is about to be deceived:

A MEANING OF SILENCE

A Seeker-after-Truth who was anxious to find a true Master saved up his money and made a long journey to the dwelling-place of a Sufi sage.

When he was admitted to the grounds of the house, the sage met him and talked for an hour or two about generalities. Since no mystical subject was mentioned, the visitor began to feel disappointed.

He stayed in the courtyard of the house, and some days later was admitted to the presence of the Sufi while he sat at his daily audience.

The visitor addressed the sage, saying: 'I have come from a great distance to enquire as to what might be the mark of a real Master, so that I might adopt such a one, should I ever find him.'

The Sufi gave him no answer at all. When the assembly broke up at nightfall, the seeker went to his lodging. Here he found that another visitor was present, and he mentioned the matter to him.

'Your disappointment, which is with the sage, should be with yourself, for failing to understand him,' said the other. 'When he talked generalities to you, he was saying that you were still fit only for generalities, and should not try to converse on any higher subject until a master initiated such converse. When, in the assembly, you received only silence to your question, you were being shown that the mark of a real master is to be able *not* to answer questions put by people who are not able to make good use of an answer already given them.'

Since I started to publish these stories in 1964, and with an ever-increasing volume of letters, cablegrams and telephone calls which is quite astonishing, people have been showing the greatest possible interest in them. The most frequent question is: 'How can I *use* teaching-stories?', and a close second is the remark, 'I get no spiritual sensations from them.' Now, the answer to these questions is really very simple, and I have often been able to get people to produce the answer themselves, by throwing the question right back at them, asking them to question their assumptions. This technique, of course, is also advocated in dozens of the published tales themselves. Then, on reflection, they answer, of course, things like 'Perhaps I have to know *more* before I can use them', and 'Spirituality to me may mean something which gives me a certain kind of emotional sensation linked with specific images. So I may have to perceive what it really is.'

A DIFFERENT KIND OF DISCIPLE

One of the specialities of the Sufis is to approach the same thing – the needs of the student – from many different directions, so that by what we call 'scatter' (a constellation of impacts), the picture ultimately comes together and he understands. Another story might make this versatility and undogmatic approach clearer:

There was once a Sufi teacher who dressed his disciples in robes of wool, had them carry begging bowls made of sea-coconuts, taught them to whirl in a mystic dance, and intone passages from certain classics.

A philosopher asked him: 'What would you do, as a Sufi teacher, if you went to a country where there were no sheep for the wool, where sea-coconuts were unknown, where dancing was considered immoral, and where you were not allowed to teach classics?'

He immediately answered: 'I would find, in such a place, a quite different kind of disciple.'

It is, in the Sufi area, the possibility of oneself becoming a quite different kind of disciple, learner or teacher, free from the tyranny of instruments, externals and dogma, which is predicated in the contention that all secondary ideas and things, among the Sufis, exist only to be dispensed with in higher ranges of education: and preferably as soon as possible.

Quite obviously, in any community there are many people who only obtain their sense of identity from such externals and appurtenances. They will not be attracted to the greater and most effective depths of teaching-stories – in fact, some are actually almost terrified by them.

Teaching-stories have been described to me, despairingly, as 'one long series of testing devices', which is only a little more useful than the phrase that 'life is only one damned thing after another'. However true it may be, is that all that can be seen by such an observer? Very possibly.

Teaching-stories, I am sure, annoy people because they will say, again and again, that you cannot treat measles by painting out the spots...

THE TESTING FUNCTION

And the testing function is certainly there. The chief feature of this testing, however, is to illustrate to the person himself what some of his major characteristics of thought are, so that he may modify them or be able to detach from them, instead of being their slave. Observing each other's reactions, too, can help a class to widen their perception of the tales.

One such story – *The Tale of the Sands* – sometimes shows people their own dependency situation, quite dramatically. In this tale the river, aware of its existence, runs towards the sea, but arrives before that at a stretch of sand, and starts to run away into nothingness, to become at best a marsh. Terrified of losing its identity, but with no real alternative, the river allows itself to be lifted up by the wind: though only after much debate and soul-searching. The wind carries it out of danger and allows it to fall, as water, safely as it precipitates against a mountain, at the other side.

Some people love this story. For others it has all the awful quality of reminding them that they must die or that they may be being asked to choose someone or something, of whom or of which they know next to nothing, of a different kind from themselves, to submit to this and to be carried away to somewhere or something of which they have no knowledge or guarantee. Do these two reactions describe the story or the people who are commenting on it?

People exposed to this story can learn a lot about themselves just by testing its effect upon their feelings...

Rather, as it were, like a radioactive tracer in the bloodstream, you can observe the effect of these stories as they work their way through the culture. Human reactions to them are so varied and so indicative of the major preoccupations of those reacting that there is a great deal of useful instruction in how people behave to be gained just by monitoring what the stories' fate has been over a period of a decade.

Brainstorming sessions have been called to crack the codes of their meaning, papers have been written on their origins and derivatives. Middle Eastern publishers have been affronted that I could make what they imagine must be a good living by publishing 'futile tales from villagers in backward areas'. Some self-styled Sufis have claimed that they knew all about them all the time but wanted to use 'more effective means', while others of the same kidney have started to teach them themselves, saying to any enquirer that they had just been waiting to get around to them. And some, of course, have been setting them as exercises to their students, teasing out strange supposed 'meanings', or saying that one must not look for any meaning at all.

NASRUDIN

The stories seem to have a magic which makes people reveal their true selves, one constantly feels. And they make a lot of things out of the academic world work. One scholar had told everyone who would listen that *I* had invented the esoteric qualities ascribed to the Mulla Nasrudin corpus. When he was told that there was an article about this by a Westerner who had studied these matters actually in the East, he instantly replied that I must have written the article myself. I am wondering what he will say when he learns that one of the earliest translations of Nasrudin in English, over a century old, speaks of this esoteric quality of what later became thought of merely as a joke-figure. He will no doubt think that I am a reincarnation of the translator of that time.

PUTTING IN AND TAKING OUT

What tends to make a fruitful approach to the tales difficult currently in the West is that the very tendencies which they are trying to describe are sometimes increased by the stories themselves. There is the same problem in the East, of course. I have heard at least twenty versions of one quip about this very subject which goes something like this:

An impatient student approached a Sufi and asked him: 'At what point will I be able to extract the meaning and make use of the content of the stories really effectively?'

The sage gave a great sigh and answered: 'At the exact point when you stop asking when you will get to that point, and put something *into* your study, instead of constantly trying to get something *out*.'

The legends which surround teaching-tales are, of course, numerous, even magical. It is widely believed, for instance, that people who repeat the Tale of Mushkil Gusha (which I have published in *Caravan of Dreams**) will attract the help of the mysterious personage Mushkil Gusha, the Remover of All Difficulties. The Nasrudin tales are under a benevolent spell. It is said that whenever one of his tales is recited, seven more will have to be repeated, because as a schoolboy he was so addicted to stories and his teacher put this hex on him. My sister, Amina Shah, has recently republished the famous Sufi book *The Tale of the Four Dervishes*** in English. The legend which goes with this book is that a Sufi master placed the benediction upon it which makes its reciting a miraculous healing procedure. But for the most part, luckily, the story-form has made the tales most usually seen as entertainment, or to be understood on their lowest level, as moral warnings. This has prevented too much mumbo-jumbo from coalescing around them.

Minor advantages have also been spontaneously observed. When I did a documentary programme for British television, I told a group of children a tale which is familiar in Central Asia, and which we used in England as part of the teaching in the children's school at our house.

THE LION WHO SAW HIS FACE IN THE WATER

There was once a lion who lived in a desert which was very windy; and because of this, the water in the holes from which he usually drank was never still, for the wind riffled the surface and never reflected anything.

---

* Idries Shah: *Caravan of Dreams*, London 1968 etc., and Baltimore (Penguin) 1972.
** Amina Shah: *The Tale of the Four Dervishes*, London 1976, 1978.

One day this lion wandered into a forest, where he hunted and played, until he felt rather tired and thirsty. Looking for water, he came across a pool of the coolest, most tempting, and most placid water that you could possibly imagine. Lions, like other wild animals, can smell water, and the scent of this water was like ambrosia to him.

So the lion approached the pool, and extended his neck to have a good drink. Suddenly, though, he saw his reflection – and imagined that it must be another lion.

'Oh dear,' he thought to himself, 'this must be water belonging to another lion – I had better be careful.'

He retreated, but then thirst drove him back again, and again he saw the head of a fearsome lion looking back at him from the surface of the pool.

This time our lion hoped that he might be able to frighten the 'other lion' away; and so he opened his mouth and gave a terrible roar. But no sooner had he bared his teeth than, of course, the mouth of the 'other' lion opened as well, and this seemed to our lion to be an awful and dangerous sight.

Again and again the lion retreated and then returned to the pool. Again and again he had the same experience.

After a long time, however, he was so thirsty and desperate that he decided to himself: 'Lion or no lion, I am going to drink from that pool!'

And, lo and behold, no sooner had he plunged his face into the water than the 'other lion' disappeared!

There was no special intention of spreading this story as a psychological support or therapeutic tool for parents with fearful children. But I got a good many letters after the TV film was shown, saying how parents had been able to use the story to reassure various youngsters who had fears of the unknown or of unfamiliar situations. It is true that these tales are told to children in the East, instead of the more gruesome ones which are often found in Hans Andersen and the Brothers Grimm; and no doubt there is a gap which could be filled here. They would be useful to children, and certainly entertain them, as we have found for many years. They are less attractive to many adults, as has been proved by the fact that the people who choose books for children, that is, adult publishers' readers, have universally turned them down as unsuitable or uninteresting, 'though' as one has kindly said, 'admittedly curious'.

The stories have become something of a rage in schools and partly through BBC educational broadcasting, where they are constantly used and widely discussed, laying down a stratum of interest which results in constant enquiries and callers from all over the place.

* * *

No account of teaching-stories can be really useful unless there has been a recital of some of these tales without any explanation at all. This is because some of the effect can be prevented by an interpretation: and the difference between an exposition and a teaching-event is precisely that in the latter nobody knows what his or her reaction is supposed to be (from any doctrinal standpoint) so that there can be a private reaction and a personal absorption of the materials. So let us look at one or two of the tales, now, under conditions of 'no explanation', so that we can observe our own reactions.

PANACEA

There are colonies of dervishes (random and not well-informed seekers) who carry out rhythmic exercises which sometimes produce mental states that they regard (in the early stages of their experimentation) as divine illumination.

Quite a lot of ordinary people, too, are attracted by this. They imagine, quite wrongly, that all dervishes are 'illuminated', and respect them.

One day, it is related, a well-meaning but ignorant Seeker-after-Truth arrived at the encampment of a group of these weirdly dressed dervishes, one of whose number was lying on the ground with his eyeballs rolled up, in an attitude of complete surrender, on his back, the very picture of total relaxation.

'I have come to share your life and experience your experiences,' said the man eagerly, to the chief of the dervishes.

'What would you like to share with us?' asked the chief.

'Allow me to share the condition and state of that recumbent dervish,' requested the visitor.

With their customary hospitality, the dervishes obliged. Forming a ring around their new friend, they helped a scorpion to sting him.

* * *

ADMIT ONE...

A dervish died, and was being questioned by the two angels who stand guard over the Gates of Paradise.

'Why should you be admitted here?'

'When I was on Earth, I was a follower of the Great Teacher Gilani...'

'Enter.'

His place was taken by the next man, who was asked the same question.

'*I* must certainly be allowed in – for I have heard what you said to the man in front of me, and *I* was the follower, at the very same time, of *three* of the Greatest Teachers.'

The angels barred his way: 'No, you will not be allowed to enter!'

'But why not?'

'Do you think that we admit people who don't know their own minds?'

* * *

MOTHS

A Sufi once established himself at a crossroads. At night he set up a very bright lamp. Not far away he lit a candle. Beside the *candle* he sat and read his books.

'There must be some secret wisdom in this,' the people of a nearby town said to one another. But they could not fathom the language of the demonstration, if such it was; nor could they penetrate the mystery of the teaching which was being offered them.

At last a group of curious citizens, unable to restrain themselves any longer, sent a deputation to ask why the Sufi had two forms of illumination, and why he had placed them in such a manner.

'Look,' he said, 'at the lamp. It is surrounded, every night, by thousands of moths. By providing that light for moths I am left in peace by them, to read by my candle. I please the moths – and keep them away from me.

'Thus it is with humanity. If everyone knew where real knowledge was, life would be chaos. As it is, people even become frenzied whenever they imagine, like the moths, that there is something which they should surround, especially if that thing is attractive to them.'

* * *

RESERVED

There was once a pretended Sufi who had attracted a fair number of disciples, but he was nothing like as successful as a genuine teacher who lived in the next town.

He made up his mind to find out what the secret formula of the real Sufi was. Disguising himself, he asked for an audience and also to be enrolled as a disciple.

The Sufi took him in, and said: 'The one and only secret for you is that you make a mixture of sugar and water and lie out in the open air without moving, smeared with it, for several hours a day. Then you will attain to the adequate truth.'

The impostor went back to his own headquarters and told all his followers to use the sugar and water exercise. Insects descended in swarms on all of them, and all the disciples abandoned him.

Eventually, lonely and eaten up with curiosity, he returned to the Sufi. 'I came to you, I now confess, to learn your secret. But, when I gave your exercise to my disciples, they were plagued by hornets and they all deserted me,' he said.

'That's how it should have been,' said the Sufi. 'The idea was that your disciples should be driven away from the impostor, and that *you* would be driven to the stage of desperation and focus upon a single problem from which alone *you* can really learn.'

* * *

WHAT TO SEE

A party of pilgrims were sitting in the presence of a great spiritual teacher when he stood up and dramatically pointed at one of them. Immediately the man fell down in an ecstasy.

When they all got back to their resthouse, this man became impatient while they were excitedly discussing the miracle of the instant illumination.

'What about me?' he demanded; 'after all, it was me he did it to!' The leader of the group looked at him with disgust. 'You seem to forget,' he said, 'that we came to see *him*, the great man, doing the illuminating – not to see *you* being illuminated!'

* * *

SURE REMEDY

A man went to visit his physician. 'My trouble is,' he told him, 'that I fall asleep during the very long lectures given by my spiritual guide.'

The doctor handed him a bottle of pills. 'One, three times a day,' he said.

'Thank you, doctor – do I take them with water?'

'No, you don't take them – in *his* food, you fool!'

* * *

UNANIMOUS

Two would-be disciples met after having visited a certain sage.

'I have decided, after listening to that man,' said the first, 'that he lacks the spiritual insights which I previously hoped would characterise him...'

'Yes,' agreed the second Seeker-after-Truth, 'he wouldn't take me on, either!'

*   *   *

Educating through the teaching-story follows many of the patterns in other kinds of instruction. For example, there will always be *some* people – very few – in any community who will be able to understand the whole body of teaching material without any instruction, without the benefit of any specialised institution to impart this knowledge to people in measured and appropriate stages. You might guess how many people would be able to do this if you were to ask yourself, as a rough analogy, how many people in a country without, say, mathematics or poetry would be able to understand the whole of such an art or science just by immersing themselves in poetry or mathematics.

From our standpoint, therefore, the question is entirely hypothetical. Besides, it might be noted, why would anyone want to re-invent mathematics? Have you enough time, apart from capacity?

For what we call education, teaching and learning, there have to be teachers, materials and learners, and these have to be in a certain kind of alignment or relationship for the optimum results to be obtained.

We can prepare the climate, introduce ideas and indicate some usages of teaching-stories in an introduction such as this. Mentioning the unfamiliarity of the concept of stories, quoting some as illustrations of part of the process, referring to how people have reacted and continue to react to them, showing barriers to using them and contending that they are indeed, highly sophisticated teaching-frames – this is what we have been doing, as a sort of gallop around some of the more easily noted relatively exterior features of this really intricate matter.

But there is no instant application of the stories as a sort of magic wand: or even as some kind of band-aid dressing.

The stories, as a body, and correctly used, offer a remarkable way into another way of thinking and of being. If they are considered only as individual items which can be adopted to add to a repertory, or for any other instantly obvious purpose, they are not much more useful than almost any other literary form intelligently used.

The whole, holistic if you like, body of material and its operation is being introduced now. I would ask you not to be satisfied with imitations. These, as I am sure you already know, are characterised by crypticism on the one hand and telling you what you want to hear on the other. No form of education I know about does that, but cults do. I can do no better than to quote at this point Rumi, one of our great masters: 'You may have a magic ring – but you must be a Solomon, master of invisible powers, to make it work.'

V   The Teaching Story – 2

UNTIL VERY RECENTLY, as you will see if you have read books on human cultures and have any acquaintance with existing groups, including religious and psychological ones, human institutions have tended to be what can only be called restrictive. That is to say, although they want to increase information and to develop capacities, they leave great areas unstudied. There is a disposition to assume that certain attitudes must not be taken up in their particular system, otherwise such attitudes might threaten the stability or even the very life of the sacrosanct institution. If you are a lawyer, you will tend to have a legalistic mind. If you have decided that certain things are for the greater social good, you will place an interdict upon working with things which appear to you at the time, at some imagined point in time, to militate against that good. The unenlightened search of the 'social good' tends to be restrictive. The result of this narrowing of the thinking is to make the person involved in it *less* effective, *more* mechanical, more prone to look for systems.

In the West, in spite of its tradition of restless exploration, we find so much folklore connected with the belief that everything is in fact examined, that it can be difficult to explain that there are things which the West does not think about. Again and again, we see that people trained within Western dogmas of all kinds try, when we get deeply into things, to relate everything which is being put forward in terms of a dogma which is already held in their minds.

Even in psychology, where things have to be rendered in the frameworks of, say, Freud or Jung, or interpersonalism, the desire for system *as understood by dogmatists* is accompanied by, or perhaps underlies, a powerful desire to establish, by association or interpretation, similarities with what they already think. This compulsion is partly, I am sure, rooted in a basic desire for order. It is also a symptom of not having shaken off the suffocating attitude of the Middle Ages, where everything had to fit in with a received, and uniformalist, view. This attitude accompanied the last two phases of human panacea thinking, where the neo-medieval systems of the Age of Reason and the Age of Technology were as restrictive and as unfruitful as the religio-scholastic one which they affected to replace.

Here is the very sharp distinction between the Sufi attitude and these compulsively pattern-seeking ones:

PATTERN-SEEKING

In the pattern-seeking approach, people will look at your materials to see which of their preconception systems they accord with. Hence, say, in Victorian British books on the Sufis, they are often represented as close to English gentlemen or sometimes as ignorant savages. Work done in the Age of Reason emphasises the Sufis as people of rationality. The people of the Age of Technology, naturally, are greatly pleased to find that Sufis are 'so modern'. Today this is one of their most frequent remarks about Sufi matters.

Now the effect of all this is that in every age only one or two possible versions of what the Sufis *are* is revealed, like the people feeling the elephant in the dark. The result of all this is, of course, that by the time you have worked through all the possible interpretations of what the Sufi way is, according to your current and local lights, it will have taken you many centuries.

Furthermore, when it is established to the satisfaction of the investigator that Sufism is, shall we say, a form of neoplatonism or of anti-clericalism or of psychology or education, he will heave a great sigh of relief. The last word has been said on the subject – the investigator can go to sleep again, having done his little bit towards making the world more comfortable by putting yet another piece of unexplained material into its duly labelled box.

The answer of the people to whom this is said, by the way, is that unless we do as best we can to reinterpret, say, Sufism, within the framework of contemporary knowledge, updating when we can, everything would be chaos, and there would be licence for people to be as woolly-headed as they liked, and science and civilisation would break down.

There are only two things wrong with this argument: both of them destroying it. The first is that the Sufis for a very considerable time have been among the most advanced people in being able to display efficiency of thought and action, and all the things that conventional achievers like to think about and pride themselves on.

This is because the Sufis can demonstrate that another mode of thinking does not destroy the mechanical, which takes its proper place as a subordinate, not a sovereign one. The intellect is not sovereign: *knowledge* is. The other error is to assume that, say, the Sufi approach might not have solved the very difficulty in which you are – that it might actually be the answer to the problem which is so often expressed as: 'How can we think about one thing in two different ways, or of two things at once?' Sufis *do* make this claim, and they are not likely to abandon it, central as it is to their whole orientation. After all, it works.

So we are, in fact, offering far more than most people interested in us are likely to want. Sufis do not offer to tinker with someone's horse and cart if they are in the business of teaching locomotion...

In this central discussion, the Sufi teaching-story has a vital place.

Instead of spending generations looking at things from the points of view of successive dogmas, the Sufi approach is to look at the materials (in this case the stories) successively if you like but from every point of view. This is why, of course, Sufis were using, centuries ago, what people today with whoops of joy identify as 'Freudian', 'Jungian' and suchlike attitudes. They discovered (and who would not if this approach were used?) the various possible attitudes towards human behaviour, and researched them without becoming hypnotised into the belief that these postures must be right as they discovered them, and building schools of belief upon them.

DIDACTIC PREVENTS UNDERSTANDING

This is because the Sufis learned very early that far from it being useful to adopt one theory after another in psychology and education, it was only after as rapidly as possible exhausting the limits by study that they could get at the truth beyond. When you have run out of theories, you will find fact. When *didactic* has been worked through, you get *understanding*.

For this reason we can clearly see the value of the exhaustive method of working with stories that I am about to outline.

The Sufi practice is to take a number of tales and ask a group of people to look at them. They then have to note down the points which interested them in the stories. Instead of magnetising themselves upon those points, they have to set them aside, and look at the points that did *not* catch their attention, and ask themselves *why they missed these*. What censorship or lack of understanding was operating? People first make their notes separately, then study them in unison, so that everyone taking part is possessed of all the reactions of the others. In this way a mosaic is built up, people all contribute, one to the other's understanding. Now a Sufi teacher goes through the results and indicates the points which nobody has noticed, which are then fed back into the minds of the group, which is able to add to its individual and collective knowledge the material which it could not provide from among its own members. When this process has been completed, one may expect a dramatic improvement in the understanding-capacity of all the people involved.

This is what we regard as proper teaching and learning. First you do what you can. Then you profit from what others are doing, and they from you. Finally you get the additional element which was absent from your own knowledge stock, provided by your teacher.

You may care to contrast this method with that of, say, theological didactic. Only the other day I visited a religious building where the cleric had so far lost the thread of teaching in any – to me – identifiable form that he was haranguing about twenty old ladies on the need to give up pornography and obscenity in their lives. He was, of course, talking to himself. But what were the qualifications, what was the insight, of this teacher at that moment?

We have in earlier pages covered no less than eighty points, ranging over the need to prepare, the absence of necessary postures before understanding teaching-stories can properly come about, the often very trivial barriers which prevent our making use of this great treasure of knowledge. These eighty statements often overlap, and some are parts of others. The published collections of tales in themselves constitute teaching-frames which make it possible to deal with some of these barriers oneself, but the purpose and existence of the instructional role and mandate is central to the whole enterprise. There are limits beyond which the familiarisation and feedback system ordinarily employed in study cannot operate without the active assistance of an instructor who is a real, not a self-appointed, one.

Sufis do not insist on the primacy of the teaching function because they want to, but because they must. It is, indeed, the Sufi's objective to render the teaching function obsolete. But first he – or she – must make available the information and the methods which are not to be found yet, for practical purposes, among the generality of the people who want to learn.

The Sufi enterprise, in which the stories can play an essential part, is to operate in areas which have been neglected. This is the Sufi contribution towards the vision of a better world.

VI   A Framework for New Knowledge...

AN ANCIENT TALE, among the Sufis, tells how a wise man once related a story about a remarkable tree which was to be found in India. People who ate of the fruit of this tree, as he told it, would neither grow old nor die. This legend was repeated, by a reliable person, to one of the Central Asian kings of long ago, and this monarch at once conceived a passionate desire for the fruit – the source of the Elixir of Life.

THE FRUIT OF THE TREE

So the King sent a suitably resourceful representative to find and to bring back the fruit of that tree. For many years the emissary visited one city after another, travelled all over India, town and country, and diligently asked about the object of his search from anyone who might know about its nature and where it was to be found.

As you can imagine, some people told this man that such a search must obviously only be a madman's quest; others questioned him closely, to find out how a person of such evident intelligence could actually be involved in such an absurd adventure; and their kindness in this respect, showing their consideration for him as a deluded dupe, hurt him even more than the physical blows which the ignorant had also rained upon him.

Many people, of course, told him false tales, sending him from one destination to another, claiming that they, too, had heard of the miraculous Tree.

Years passed in this way, until the King's representative lost all his hope of success, and made the decision to return to the royal court and confess his dismal failure.

Now, there was also, luckily, a certain man of real wisdom in India – they do occasionally exist there – and the King's man, having heard of him late in his search, thought: 'I will at least go to him, desperate as I am, to seek his blessing on my journey homeward…'

He went to the wise man, and asked him for a blessing, and he explained how it was that he had got into such a distressed condition, a failure without hope.

The sage laughed and explained: 'You simpleton; you don't need a blessing half as much as you need orientation. *Wisdom* is the fruit of the Tree of Knowledge. Because you have taken images and form, secondary names for things, as your aim, you have not been able to find what lies beyond. It has thousands of names: it may be called the Water of Life, the Sun, an Ocean and even a Cloud… But the emblem is not the thing itself.'

Whoever, this Teacher continued, attaches himself to names and clings to concepts without being able to see that these derivative things are only stages, sometimes barriers, to understanding, will stay at the stage of secondary things. They create, and remain in, a subculture of emotional stimulus, fantasy and quasi-religion.

COMMUNITY ASSUMPTIONS

You will observe, as the Sufis strenuously maintain, that this principle holds good even in easily grasped conditions of human life. If you belong to a community which has made certain assumptions about life and society, and even knowledge, you will find that the community constitutes a stable entity so long as it does not question its basic assumptions. This may inhibit progress.

In New Guinea it has been observed not only that the head-hunting system worked to virtually everyone's satisfaction, but also that, when threatened by different moral values from outside, it disintegrated. When, for instance, young men seeking a bride were forbidden to carry out the custom of lopping off an enemy's head and were thus prevented from taking it – as proof of their manliness – as an offering to their intended father-in-law, they suffered what was indistinguishable from what we call guilt and remorse. In their context it *was* guilt and remorse.

In any society stabilised upon a whole range of interlocking assumptions, many of which really do seem to verify one another, there is a sense of coherence and strength which is naturally highly prized by its members. This is, of course, because the individuals are not autonomous enough to be alone for long. This desire to identify oneself by group-association is so strong that when one social grouping breaks down it is normal for it to be succeeded by another ideology offering similar facilities for reassurance and an adequate world-view. This is the familiar story of national and cultural history. It has its parallels in the individual. When someone's ideas begin to provide a less-than-adequate support for his sense of individual integrity and group cohesion, we get a reshaping of them around a new or improved concept: again, if he or she is not psychologically autonomous. It is dissatisfaction and insecurity, a sense of the need for something, which is often described as more 'real' or 'true', which precedes the condition known as conversion-syndrome, just before the restabilisation which I have just mentioned. Members of dependency-oriented cultures consequently find themselves vastly preoccupied by the search for comfort and reassurance, which they don't *need*: they are just used to it.

Sufi psychology recognises two important elements in this situation. First, that in order to advance in knowledge or effectiveness, people have to break bonds which prevent them from reaching development and vision. These may include immature reliance on too much totemism. You must conceive of possibilities beyond your present state if you are to be able to find the capacity to reach towards them. If you think that knowledge or long life is a tree, you may literally look for a tree if you want these things. If you believe that, say, your desires can be reached through the framework of a system in which you live or think, you will be able only to obtain the results which that society or system can accord you. Secondly, the Sufis recognise that flexibility of approach is needed, not reprogramming of beliefs.

This may all seem very obvious, once stated. But it is one of the characteristics of our time that people do *not* on the whole find it obvious enough to base their objectives or lives on it. And most of them don't conceive that such autonomy is good or even possible. The consequence is considerable confusion.

EXCLUSION OF POSSIBILITIES

The fact is, of course, that for practical purposes *all* systems which exist for furthering a purpose also succeed, almost by definition, in excluding many other possibilities: unless *you* add the extra dimensions – the system won't. You may make a lot of money in a business, but this can be at the expense of developing your interests in other directions. If you go in for clinical research, you may not be able to do as much therapy as otherwise might be possible. If you need the social support given you by any kind of a system to which you belong to an extreme degree, you will be inhibited from leaving it, even temporarily, in order to do things in areas where there is no social support: thus reducing your effectiveness. Speaking candidly, this means that you will be unable to go forward because your needs command you to spin on your own axis to maintain some kind of equilibrium. You may be a seeker, but you can never be a finder, unless the seeking is effective enough.

Faced with a situation like this, the Sufi diagnosis has for centuries been clear and unequivocal. It says that man 'finds himself', if he would only accept it, not in any static world or society, but in environments which only *look* like this. He does not live very long, he can control very little of his circumstances, and the things which happen to him, even in the most highly structured environments, may have far more effect on his life than the things which he causes to happen: however much he may strive, and irrespective of whether or not he believes the reverse to be true. Hence, in order to function more effectively, he must be versatile and flexible, not regarding transient things as constants: treating, rather, transience as if it were the constant. This concept transfers his vulnerability beyond lesser and capricious things. Because of it he can transcend limitations which otherwise paralyse or manipulate him.

This is, you will note, very far from what people imagine to be the Eastern conception of society as static, or humanity as the helpless, unambitious tool of fate. The Sufi would say, on the other hand, that people who believe in the reality of absolutes, even the absolutes widely accepted in the West, make themselves prisoners, people who find it difficult to adjust even when Nature plays tricks which affect, say, the economy in a way more far-reaching than any human intervention. Western scientists are only just starting to proclaim the relativity of absolutes, naturally as their own discovery – as, indeed it is, as far as they know.

So you could say that the Sufi dominates his environment by being able, when necessary, to stand aside from it, allowing it to have only the minimum effect on him, and by meshing with it, when indicated; while the individual (especially in the West) very often tries to dominate it by thrusting all his weight against it, marshalling every form of energy he can think of. The one attitude has largely produced the Western world, the other, much of the Eastern. But in mutual usefulness they are not as far apart as one might imagine.

SCIENCE AND REALITY

What *have* these two approaches yielded? The Western people have specialised for some centuries in dealing with material life, yet they have arrived at a point where they are more and more interested in the non-material. They are less and less able, indeed, to distinguish the one from the other. Similarly, after specialising in the study of man for about the same number of centuries, the Sufis long ago began to display what seemed to Westerners, and still do, equally paradoxical interests in scientific matters.

Let us now juxtapose two pieces of information, to fix this in our minds:

We all know about the materialistic and hard-nosed attitudes of pure science towards religion – the area of the Sufis' major public form of research and expression – especially in the mystical experience of a cosmic Reality. Albert Einstein, however, arrived at an interesting point when he said:

The cosmic religious experience is the strongest and the noblest driving force behind scientific research.*

To what extent was he typical of the way in which scientific thought is going?

Well, Dr Evan Harris Walker, an eminent theoretical physicist, is on record as saying recently:

It now appears that research under way offers the possibility of establishing the existence of an agency having the properties and characteristics ascribed to the religious concept of God.**

And the Sufis, whom your encyclopaedias are almost sure to define (by simplistic suppression of much of the materials about them) as Islamic ecstatics, dancing dervishes, monks and so on, have been baffling many outward students of religion for at least 1,000 recorded years by discussing, in texts continuously extant and which are yet notionally religious documents, the most astonishingly 'modern' things, without any identifiable technical instrumentation or scientific infrastructure to explain how they knew of them. These include space-travel, atomic power, time–space theory, the circulation of the blood, a fourth dimension, aviation, the transmission of pictures to panels set in walls – and human evolution. They do not stop at these, and telepathy, telekinesis, penetrating physical objects under paradoxical circumstances, and instant learning by holistic methods are only a few of the subjects which they have insisted on, from ancient times, as realities which also accord with contemporary Western

*   Albert Einstein, quoted in his Obituary, 19 April 1955.
** The *Observer* (London), 20 February 1972 ('Sayings of the Week').

interest and attempted investigation; but which they insist are concomitants of, but not ways to, spiritual knowledge.

It really does seem to me that it is scientific thinking as much as anything else which has led people in the West recently to look for mental activity in more ancient cultures which have specialised in it, for possible information, especially of concept and method, which might accord in some way with current Western hypotheses; and this has led them in the past few years to the Sufis; whose field seems, even if we only compare this roughly, to accord in its alleged results with what Western workers think that they might find – supposing there really to be a tradition of Eastern psychology sufficiently intact and legitimate to have preserved suitable indications of local and cosmic interactions.

NEW LEARNING FROM THE PAST

Psychologists have been interested to note that Sufi tradition a thousand years ago insisted that human beliefs are frequently produced and sustained by the environment, by the culture, and that what people call 'belief' is not that which can really be ascribed only to divine or diabolical activity, but may be caused by conditioning, and in such cases is not 'spiritual' but induced. The Sufi development of that theme, however, building into its psychological procedures methods of ensuring that people are aware of their own conditioned responses and that belief-systems are generally therefore secondary, as a means of giving them extra capacities – this is a field not yet entered by the West, though it is trembling on its borders.

For my own part, I am particularly impressed by a new awareness, among Western thinkers and researchers, of the Eastern principle that certain pursuits, such as the Sufi one, cannot be studied from outside to any significant extent. This concept is central to Sufi ideas, and is at last becoming widely accepted elsewhere.

Even ten years ago, it was not uncommon among scholars to hear them say – as I have heard said – in answer to this claim of Sufis, that 'A stone is not as much of an authority on minerals as is a geologist'. We may laugh now, but there are still a few corners in which this assumption (that even the people from whom one wants to learn something may be unaware of what it really is) lingers. I don't say that the boot is now on the other foot, but...Sufi study is participation study, not something you learn *about*, but something which teaches you...

As with any relatively 'new' learning, some of the principles may be understood better than others by those who want to examine them, depending upon their preparation. There is a real danger that individual pieces of Sufi information, technique or the like, simply fed into the existing Western frameworks, employed, that is, by conventional minds, in inadequate contexts, could succeed only in acting on a much lower level than a comprehensive handling of the materials requires. The results of this do-it-yourself approach are not worth bothering with. Many Indian gurus have, however, done this, both in India and in the West.

I think that it is well worth remembering that the introduction of new knowledge is far more difficult – and so is its sustaining – than the commercialising, as it were, of portions of it, in formats not really suitable for its activity – however admirable they might be in their own way. Even quite distinguished psychologists, too often for *my* liking, still ask me for 'a bit of Sufi psychology to work with'. If you can't work with it by reason of lacking background, even the whole, let alone a bit, is essentially useless, except to play with.

Once upon a time, goes the story which casts some light upon this tendency, there was a beggar who went up to a rich man and asked him for the price of a cup of coffee. The magnate handed him a high-denomination banknote, and said:

'Take this, it's enough for twenty cups of coffee', and each went his way.

The following day, the rich man saw the beggar again, and asked him how he had got on.

'You and your twenty cups of coffee,' said the beggar in disgust, 'they kept me awake all night!' It is not made easier to enunciate this fact of the need for preparation when people (as they so often do in the West) imagine that you are not being descriptive but accuse you of condescension...

This proclivity, the random adoption of Sufi ideas and exercises, is already in almost full cry in many countries, and some of the less desirable results are quite visible. There is no real harm done, by the way, in the mimicry of Sufi ways, or the dressing in comic Eastern clothes, or even the imagining that certain chants and symbols and caperings will bring higher states of awareness, providing, of course, that the society is free and therefore also allows the actual facts to be known. The facts being that anyone who thinks that he can get higher consciousness by jumping up and down or performing circus acts or adopting instrumental exercises as magic keys – or even by merely listening to, consuming, such material as this – is so obviously only amusing himself (or herself) that sensible people, both Sufis and others, must see that this is relatively harmless. But to be only a harmless self-amuser when one believes oneself to be involved in cosmic affairs is surely absurd or even tragic.

There is a famous Sufi story which clearly sets forth the two levels of religion, the one of observance and social concern, and the other, of higher psychological import, generally called the *Tale of Moses and the Shepherd*,* and written by the great thirteenth century Sufi, Rumi:

OBSERVANCE VERSUS KNOWLEDGE

Moses came upon a shepherd who was praising God and saying, aloud, that he wanted to serve him by mending his sandals and combing his hair, to wash his clothes and bring him milk, and much more in the same vein.

Now Moses, incensed at the foolishness and familiarity of this simple man, approached and charged him with blasphemy and ravings. The shepherd humbly accepted the rebukes and went off into the desert.

Then, the tale continues, an inspiration came from above to Moses, telling him that he had separated this man from his idea of God, for each stage of humanity has its own relative conceptual frameworks; that the figurative expression did not matter: what was essential was the reality. So Moses ran into the wilderness and found the shepherd again, and told him that his idea of religion *was* acceptable to God, and that there was nothing wrong in everyone imagining something which was ordinarily imperceptible by means of his own kind of imagery, to satisfy the level of his condition.

This, of course, is intended to illustrate that the satisfactions obtained through one's own level of understanding are indeed legitimate, and there is no point in disturbing a stability of mind without anything more advanced being, for some reason, able to replace it.

And yet the story has a further sequel. The shepherd now turned to Moses and assured him that it was the shock of

---

* *The Mathnawi*, Book II (Rumi).

being told how superficial he was that had, in the ensuing time, enabled the shepherd to rise to higher truths. 'I am now,' he continued, 'in a state where I am beyond images and imagery...according to the loftiness of your aspiration, so will be the increase of your capacity to transcend lesser ideas.'

In this story, then, we see at least three stages in the Sufi psychological system.

When the Sufi knows what a person *really* believes and what he or she *really* wants, he can tell whether Sufi knowledge will be of any use to that person or not: and in what form the attempted communication is to be couched. Does this would-be learner first have to learn how to learn? When the would-be Sufi has a similar idea of his real situation, he will be able to feel two things: *one*, whether he really wants Sufi understanding; and *two*, he will be able to sense, rather than to imagine, the Sufic current, the 'call' as it is termed, which is shut out of one's awareness by coarser ambitions and preoccupations. Very many of the accepted socio-psychological preoccupations imagined to be of a higher order are in fact only the indulgence in those coarser, but quite legitimate, pursuits.

Sufi literature, particularly the portions which I have selected and published in over a dozen books for this specific purpose, is designed, at least in part, to help show a person's real state to himself.* It is because of the forthright nature of this material, which is after all a textbook and an instrumental corpus, not entertainment, that the Sufis are imagined, by the malobservation of insensitive minds, to set out to deflect, by means of intractable behaviour, the attachment of those who are most easily deterred. Such assessments consequently fail

* See my *Tales of the Dervishes* and *The Magic Monastery*.

to appreciate the importance of such instructions as this, by Hakim Jami, the great poet (who died in 1492):

Beguzar az laf-i-aql, ki hast
Aql inja akkala, wa fazl fuzul

(Abandon boasting of intellect and learning, for here intellect is corrosive, and learning is foolishness.) He is speaking, of course, of what passes for intellection and wisdom among the shallow.

The great Sufi poet Hafiz of Shiraz (fourteenth century) constantly emphasises, as what we would today call a psychological exercise, that man's preoccupations prevent him from making progress in the realm of a higher consciousness. He sits, as it were, surrounded by screens, blocking off his appreciation of his own potentiality. Limited thinking, however useful for limited purposes, 'veils' human potential:

Tu khud hijab i khudi Hafiz
Az miyan bar-khez!

He says: 'You yourself are your own screen, Hafiz / rise from its midst!' This screen, of course, can sometimes be composed of the very research concepts adopted to study the Sufi phenomenon by self-imagined Sufis. This is why, as in the East, the rise of a Western questioning of its own limiting assumptions is so important.

It is, of course, not impossible to find, in this and other societies, people who already understand that, while there may be levels of perception, knowledge and understanding *beyond* those which they currently enjoy, yet they are satisfied to remain in the mental, physical and cultural context in which their stimulus-needs are satisfied. It is the ones who don't know their true situation, however, who are more numerous and vocal. It is very often *they* who have the least possibility of liberating themselves from the bonds of their assumptions, though they often imagine themselves to be seekers after Truth...

Such a person was the shepherd in the Moses story, until Moses came along. If you can be sure that your 'shepherd' will be stimulated, and not broken, by such shocks as Moses gave his, you will be in a position to tell people that they *should* have higher consciousness. But you may have to help them to understand that it may very well be the last thing that they need in their present adequate integration into their society, if they lack the flexibility to be '*in* the world, not *of* it'. Real seeking is far more adventurous – and more profitable – than such people really know.

That is the difference, in a nutshell, between the missionary and the Sufi. The one has to make converts, the other is able to teach only those who really want to learn. Before this happens, both parties in the latter (but not the former) process have to be thoroughly aware that this really *is* the situation. The instructor must be able to diagnose the stage of his pupil, the learner must come to the stage where he can accept this.

If there is any definition of a real Sufi teacher, it must include that he can tell the difference between entertainment and instruction, between circus and teaching; between didactic and action, between awareness-teaching and therapy. The imitation spiritual teacher or student may well believe, as do many thousands of them even today, some not a million miles from here, that being a source of worship or comfort to someone else is a spiritual activity, not a social or emotional one. This does not make this delusion the truth, however many people it convinces of its truth...

So, being able to tell one thing from another is an essential quality of the Sufi. Not all things, but essential ones. He does not mix human comfort with teaching for the same reason that he might not mix any two things together which work more effectively when concentrated upon as themselves, and not as a part of some arbitrarily assumed whole. On the contrary, the Sufi is aware that it is by the very capacity to see things for what they are, and for their hindering as well as helping effect, that he can maintain Sufi activity in what is, speaking in terms of physics, almost a hostile environment. That this does not make him less spiritual or human than anyone else is proved – if it has to be – by the fact that in the East the Sufis are recognised by people of all faiths as among the greatest saints and servants of humanity, without dispute.

SIMPLIFICATION

It certainly is my own experience that when real Sufi definitions are made and understood, the understanding of the Sufi development and path by the student become enormously easier. But we may have to wait until enough psychologists and other researchers want higher consciousness more than they need emotional stabilisation, or elegant monographs to their names, for there to be significant numbers willing to undertake this higher range of real Sufi study. And a consequent widespread availability of this kind of knowledge.

As a piece of applied psychology, it is worth noting that people who want Sufi ideas simplified for them do *not*, in frequently repeated experience, show an increase in understanding following such simplification. And yet, if they are first taught Sufi exercises enabling them to concentrate better, they do not need any intellectual activity such as breaking-down of elusive concepts into simplistic grotesques or penny packets to understand them with relative ease. You might say that it is not always wise to ask the patient to prescribe for himself, especially if you are a doctor. Similarly, before assuming that you are talking too softly, as someone may claim, also investigate whether he needs to wash out his ears. Teaching, one must repeat, is to give what the learner really needs...

You may have heard the story which puts in a nutshell the distortion and failure to communicate which many attempts at simplification can produce:

A certain Sufi was in the habit of making what seemed to his hearers to be disjointed utterances. He did this because it was through just such behaviour that he had himself learned from his own teacher, and because he was trying to communicate with a conventionally minded scholar. But the scholar could make no sense of what the Sufi was saying, or doing, or whatever was going on. He constantly begged him to be more specific, to describe his experiences lucidly, to delineate the truths which he saw with far greater precision, and so on.

Our kind-hearted mystic – uncharacteristically for his trade, but necessarily for the development of this story – tried, and tried, and tried. Finally, when his thoughts were verbally marshalled in the most organised way imaginable, he wrote it all down. This long, impassioned but grammatical account of his deepest experiences was sent, together with a sketch of the whole manner of its attaining, to the scholar.

The manuscript came back next day from the desk of the man of learning, with this comment written upon it:

'The admitted increase in your ability to express yourself has, however, only succeeded in revealing the inadequacies of your logic.' The scholar was not ready to see that the Sufi was showing him what happened to instrumental material reprocessed into logic.

The Sufi assertion is that the teacher, the teaching and the taught must be in harmony *and* in alignment; otherwise only distortions leading to a cult or other low-level stabilisation are most likely to be the result. The cultists, both in East and West, although they have access to the classical and authoritative Sufi texts giving these warnings, suppress them.

With the Sufi way, its psychology-in-action requires that certain exercises, such as concentration and also diffusion of attention, for instance, must be kept in balance.

HOW, WHEN AND WITH WHOM

A major factor additional to the need to prepare the learner for the mystical experience which takes forms not yet even noted in the West, is that of how, when and where, and with whom, the necessary development may be carried out. The consciousness must be attuned in accordance with a knowledge of the possibilities. This is what distinguishes real, traditional Sufi teaching from the forms in which exercises are just handed out randomly. An Indian story illustrates this need for proper measure in psychology, as in nutrition:

It is about a man who went to a restaurant and ordered curry and rice. It was a long time coming, and as he was very hungry he asked what was holding things up. 'Well, sir, the curry is ready, but the rice is not.'

'Very well,' he said, 'bring me the curry to start on, and I'll have the rice later.'

They brought the curry, but he was so hungry that he had finished it up before the rice arrived. As he ate his way through the plain boiled rice, when it did come, he found it hard going, and he asked for some more curry to go with it. So they started to cook some more curry, but of course by the time it was ready the rice was eaten up, and he had to order more rice to go with that: the curry was hot. Before the two elements, as it were, got into phase, he hated the sight of both curry and rice.

Apart from the quite imaginable correspondence of the rice with the left hemisphere of the brain and the curry with the right, I invoke this tale to say to you that the Sufi way of thought has been called 'too structured' by some and 'insufficiently coherent' by others. And invoke it to emphasise that curry and rice complement one another: and *that* principle is central to Sufi work.

To the Sufi, failure to observe this is equivalent to the behaviour of someone who blames a surgeon as inconsistent because he had been observed sometimes to take things out of a human body and sometimes to put things in....

It is partly due to this special usage of techniques, through 'feel' and not slavishly by a textbook – as well as the relative shortcomings of the surrounding culture's information-stock – that many confusing legends in many countries developed about Sufis over the centuries. Both these factors and also the numerous imitators and self-imagined 'Sufis' have, since the earliest recorded times in this tradition, muddled the public's understanding of the Sufi. But the Sufis have always survived it. Indeed, they are able to make use of it by contrasting primitive and sensationalist thought and activity with the real thing, as I am doing at this very moment....

There are many other factors which Sufi knowledge indicates as barriers to learning and also many which distinctly facilitate it. That some of this material is put into poetry, into teaching-tales or embodied into actual instructional situations or records of them, does not make the study any easier for people who are unfamiliar with these modes of presentation as containing a dynamic – not just to be consumed. Teaching-stories, for instance, require careful interaction-study as part of a comprehensive course, constantly monitored to assess progress and to encourage it, if their usefulness is to be exploited beyond a certain point.

Our publishing, over the past ten years, of several hundreds of these stories has ensured their wide currency for entertainment. It has also enabled us to contact those who have appreciated inner dimensions in them without the need for further work. The attempt, by opportunists, to build them into various existing systems and esoteric philosophies, has stimulated the questions as to how they really *are* to be employed – which has enabled us to prepare for the next stage in this psychological enterprise. They cannot just be adopted and fed into arbitrary frames. We have deliberately held back from premature interpretation, to frustrate the pirating of the material by incompetents and worse.

THEMES AND CULTURAL CONTEXT

The *system* of the Sufis, if I can use that word for it, is constantly manifested in different forms in accordance with local cultures. It is not regarded as the consequence of research, but as the application of experience to specific conditions. The Sufi experience is, to the Sufi, cosmic and hence extradimensional: humanity having the capacity to perceive that which is beyond the range of conventionally experienced physics. But, since the Sufi has the experience, he can devise the means of returning to it, and – if he is a teacher, which is not invariable – of helping others along the same way.

In Sufi literature, the theme of the search or *journey* is one usual convention, whether in the form of a caravan of souls, or of a lover, or of a Seeker-after-Truth. In Sufi school situations, these materials are themselves transcended as the aspirants get behind and beyond the significance of the symbolism which successively helps and then can hinder if retained too long. The system is thus very similar to the situation where you may march on a visible point, in order to keep in a straight line, only to abandon it when it has fulfilled its function, choosing another and if necessary yet another, until the goal is reached.

The experience is not only one of self-realisation, but one which enables the Sufi to understand what elements in this earthly abode of relative truth may conduce towards enlightenment. The real thing is brought back into the world, and rendered in approximate, but effective, terms. The Perfect, according to Sufis, exists in other dimensions than our own; but its local form, an approximation, leading us to it, is manifested everywhere. Hence such sayings among the Sufis as: 'Ordinary love is the temporal equivalent of Real love', and 'The created is the indication of the Creator'. The scientist or other researcher, of course, may often have a similar attitude when his motivation is to start with what is known or seen, and he works backwards to its earlier phases, even, if he can, to its origin.

The deep desire of the human being, so often seen, to seek the origin of all, is, of course, held to be due to the fact 'everything returns to its origin'.*

* * *

Jalaluddin Rumi, seven hundred years ago, wrote a poem in which he speaks of the evolution of man and the development through which he may rejoin his origins, an evolution which is a path 'retraced' as one might call it, by pushing his consciousness forward by the *exclusion* of limiting factors and the *inclusion* of others; to a destiny which is generally referred to as 'beyond the stars':

---

* *Kullu shayin yarjiu ala aslihi* is the dictum in Arabic.

ABOVE THE SKIES...

We are above the skies and *more* than angels...
Although we have descended here, let us speed
   back: what place is this?
Every form you see has its archetype in the
   placeless...
From that instant when you came down into the
   world as it is
('of being')
Placed before you to get out was a ladder.
First you were mineral, afterwards vegetable
What you then became was animal, although this
   is hidden from you.
From that you became humankind, with
   knowledge, intellect
and belief;
After this Earth, from then your place is the
   sky...*

This has delighted the flying-saucer people, whose position you will be able to judge from my earlier remarks about early and facile stabilisation of systems...

Sufi psychology, then, can only function in the presence of an awareness of the unity of all Creation, and of Creation with all existence, and all existence with something eternal.

It need not, and perhaps should not, be denied that the words and actions of the Sufis have always alluded to a cosmic plan, of which humanity is a part. Human communities are

---

* *Selected Poems from the Divani Shamsi Tabriz*, by Jalaluddin Rumi, Persian text ed. R. A. Nicholson, Cambridge University Press, 1952. Translation by Idries Shah.

seen as a part of that plan; religions as instruments of the plan; yet all forms of knowledge are admitted as related, more or less directly, to the same plan. The role of the Sufi (and the Sufi is the name for the realised man or woman, not for the mere Seeker After Truth) – you can't have a Sufi who is still learning any more than all medical students are doctors – is seen as nothing less than an instrument of the plan: but as a conscious instrument, not as a well-wisher or hero, not as a follower or optimist, not as an idealist or even as a dedicated monk.

HIGHER CONCEPTS

His role is naturally sometimes put in very dramatic form; he is the human being who is capable of being independent of fear of loss and desire for gain alike; such a person alone, it is insisted, can discharge functions which would be completely beyond the ordinary person, trapped by the stick and carrot of familiar existence. He – or she – has wider choices – though often in different areas – than other people.

This kind of thinking, naturally enough, is heartily disliked by those who trade only in reward and punishment, or who believe that ignorance is man's lot and even, some of them, that hope and fear alone are his glory. These are, however, the people and states of mind whom the Sufi sees as the barrier between man's potential and his actual state, and who, in turn, imagine (against the evidence, it must be stated) that the Sufi enterprise is one motivated by delusions of grandeur or a desire for power. They point to this kind of poem, which hits at lesser aspirations and hints at a greater, ordinarily almost undreamt-of function of humankind:

In cell and cloister, in monastery and synagogue:
Here one fears hell, another dreams of paradise.
But whoever knows the true secrets of his God –
Has planted no such seeds within his heart.

(Omar Khayyam)

This is enough to set the superficialists off into orgies of accusations of irreligion against the Sufis.

In one passage – though it is far from being the only one on this subject – Rumi in just a few lines makes the following statements, quite unusual, as I think you will agree, for seven hundred years ago:

- Humanity is sprung from the sea
- Humanity belongs above the skies
- Having descended to Earth, he must try to return
- He should not waste time on what are really circuses
- There is a continuous sound or tone, or call, calling one back.

Each of these statements is interesting, each has a use: but all belong to the technical, not the narrative, literature...

The Sufi must be able to alternate his thought between the relative and the Absolute, the approximate and the Real.

A major item in Sufi thought, therefore, is that there is an Absolute from which ordinarily perceptible things are to be regarded as local concretisations. This is why to attach oneself to secondary things, and to be unable to detach, inhibits potentiality to progress towards perception of this Absolute. This, in short, is encapsulated in the Sufi aphorism: *Al mujazu qantarat al Haqiqa* – 'The Relative is a channel to the Truth'.

INTERPLAY

One of the interesting possibilities before us, due to the recent advance in knowledge of the tendency to hemispheric specialisation in the brain, is that in its concepts we have a language in which to express things which we did not have before. Until recently, the balancing of the supposed opposite activity of the intellect and emotions answered well enough: and we still can use those metaphors for many purposes. With the awareness that many intellectual activities are, indeed, *linked* with emotions, and that emotional activity is also affected by intellection, this language has become less useful. The two-mode-brain theory is useful as a hypothesis from which one can go further, certainly in the interplay of the more or less specific and the relatively abstract.

The stimulus of the holistic mode of the brain is undoubtedly something which can be assigned to certain Sufic procedures, and so also can stimuli which might be applied to the sequential side. Let us look, as an example, at 'specialised poetry' as used by the Sufis.

If we ignore, for the moment, the 'shock' effect – in the cultural sense – of the irreligious sentiments seemingly being expressed here by the great saint Jalaluddin Rumi, we can see the driving, almost, of the holistic, image-forming part of the brain through the unusual employment of the verbal-analytical side, in this piece of poetry (in Persian it is many times more powerful in its artistic quality), where sound, and symbol and feeling are so powerfully brought together:

'How is this to be handled, O Muslims?' he says, 'For I do not know myself. Neither Christian, nor Jew am I, not Fire-Worshipper nor Muslim. Neither Easterner nor Westerner, not of the land or of the sea... Not of this world nor of the next, neither of

Heaven or of Hell…my place is placeless, my aim
is without aim…There is no body, there is no soul;
for I am *from* the Soul of Souls…'*

Though seemingly linear in expression, the effect could
hardly be more un-linear.

THE SHOCK ELEMENT

Outward formulation, as Rumi seeks to emphasise here,
however valuable in some ways, is not the essence of Truth.
The 'shock' element, in which (in a highly structured and
devout society such as we do not often see nowadays) he
denies all customary attachments, cries out for that which
lies beyond the assumed essentials, the accepted norms, the
unexamined conventional wisdoms, the things people try to
hold onto, believing them to be ultimates – or to be suitable
substitutes for ultimates.

This message, in action and in the Sufi situation, does
indeed have this effect. What it succeeds in doing, of course,
when read by merely formal thinkers or literalists – that
covers most people – is to make them imagine that he does
not know what he is doing, that he is an apostate, or that he
is making poetry by rhyming without regard to the meaning
of words. When it is indulged in just to shock oneself or
others, it has no Sufic psychological effect, however clever or
progressive it is imagined to be.

When I want a good laugh, I sometimes pick up one or
other of the academic monographs in which someone tries to

---

* Jalaluddin Rumi: *Divan of Shams-i-Tabriz*, Persian text, in R. A. Nicholson,
  op. cit., p. 124. Translation by Idries Shah.

work out 'at what stage in Rumi's spiritual development he went through the phase of irreligion'.

And yet such quotations as this – and its scholastic or amateur echoes – form only a fragment of the huge Sufi range of ideas, and hence the raw material of learning in an authentic Sufi atmosphere.

The tremendous quantity and variety of the accretions to Sufi matters which have occurred during the past thousand years or so alone have thus naturally built up, here and there, a massively distorted picture of who the Sufis are and what they have been doing and saying. This situation has, indeed, gone so far that, as I have already mentioned elsewhere, there are parts of the East in which the amazing eccentricities and extravagant misunderstandings of Sufi thought and practice by self-appointed interpreters have fathered shallow, mimetic organisations which are so powerful in their effect on the mass mind that they are actually imagined to be the real thing by the most sincere people who have had no opportunity to learn the real facts. Luckily, this is almost always only in localised forms, and any overall study of the literature, on the part of people prepared to take the trouble – few people do – easily shows that these admittedly dramatic but quite misleading groups cannot contain what *we* call Sufis, or be carrying on the Sufi studies of the classical literature and viable schools, and their extension into the present day, in a Sufic manner.

IMITATION SUFIS

The main reason why the more visible so-called 'Sufi' circuses exist is, in addition to public demand, the fact that most authentic Sufis actually avoid, as far as possible, display, or talking about secrets, or flamboyance. Neither are they concerned with the wearisome, semi-occultist didactic of so many writers on Sufism today. 'The teacher,' as one major exponent of Sufism has said, 'is one who abandons ceremonial and religious display and social appearances, and concentrates on *real* development.'*

Since the Sufi uses all legitimate means to bring his experiences and teaching usefully to people who will be able to accept it, in the most truly effective manner, he may be next to invisible to people expecting a high-profile presentation. The saying has it: 'What the self-imagined mystic seeks only in his meditation is visible to the Sufi on every street corner and in every alleyway.'**

Add to this even the minor additional element of the traditional behaviour of Sufis, that 'Some of them dress well and eat delicious food, to annoy and deflect superficialists, those who judge shallowly, by appearances',*** as equally authentic tradition has it, and you may understand *why* the Sufi is said to be more deeply hidden, in effect, than anything on earth. He wants to shake you off, if you judge by externals – and he has all the ways in the world of doing it…

This, too, is why the continuity of real Sufi understanding today is just as operative as it ever was. Our own experience makes nonsense of the oft-repeated question from the always abundant limited thinkers who ask where the Sufi giants disappeared to, and why they are not produced today. This question is legitimate only if you accept the assumption that the Sufis must necessarily be towering personalities on the skyline, or oddities of any kind: and are what Sufism is supposed to be producing constantly, instead of people

---

*   *Irshadat* of Sh. Ibrahim Gazur-i-Ilahi.

**   Ibid.

*** Ibid.

serving mankind, whether publicly or otherwise, whether labelled as Sufis or not.

There is probably no stronger evidence of selective study, or institutionalised thick-headedness, than the fact that those who worship personalities and crave their re-appearance should ignore what some of the greatest of them said on this subject: 'Do not look at my outward shape, but take what is in my hand' (Rumi); and 'The requirement in a teacher is not that he should look important and do miracles: it is that he should have what the disciple needs' (Ghazzali). If you are in awe of him, you cannot learn, any more than if you discount him. The Sufi insistence is, in current language, upon the difference between the showman and the educator, the emotionalist and the achiever. The achiever, here, of course means the effective person, not necessarily the 'man of achievement' in presently fashionable professions.

That the Sufi can in fact continue to operate without beating the big drum is useful, of course, at times and places where repressive systems curtail freedom of thought or expression; and this is indeed still the position in some countries today. And open societies which demand their educational intake only through simplistic formulae, are also repressive of progress in learning anything beyond their accepted aims.

Secondly, when the culture is in a *phase*, also recurring, in which it welcomes and encourages what are, effectively, mainly entertainers and stimulators of emotion or linear intellect (whether linked notionally with religion or psychology or not) the Sufi's ordinarily undramatic, carefully articulated operation and procedures will attract correspondingly little interest. They will be carried out privately, and you will not locate it through the occultist grapevine.

It is only recently that conditions in some countries have stabilised sufficiently for the Sufi to get a hearing for his ideas right across the board from reasonable numbers of rational people not discouraged by his references to what have more often than not been unfashionable ideas. Quite a number of Western thinkers have, indeed, been observant – and generous – enough to state that much present-day interest in the Sufis is based on what one of them has called 'greed, not hunger, for knowledge'.

This, then, is something of the framework. In order to see how it can be related to contemporary questions, I propose to take a very short look at some of the historical, literary, cross-cultural and other evolutions of the Sufi teaching. Then we will return to those parts of the Sufi interest in human psychology which can in fact be dealt with in a more sequential manner.

* * *

HISTORY AND THE SUFIS

Considerations of Sufism very often begin with the question, and its attempted answer:

How did Sufism arise, and what is it rooted in?

According to historical documents, it is attributed to three sources, which many Sufis themselves have stated are essentially different manifestations of the same, extradimensional, cosmic and divine impulse. Here they are:

1. Sufism has been known under many names, to all peoples, from the beginning of human times;
2. It was, for instance, transmitted by the Prophet Muhammad to his disciple and son-in-law, Ali, and to others, thirteen hundred years ago, as the inner component of all religion;

3. It also persisted, side by side with the Prophetic transmission, as, for instance, in the independent witness of the historical figure of Uways al-Qarni, a contemporary of the Prophet who, however, never met him.*

A thousand years ago, however, Al-Hujwiri, in the first Persian treatise on the Sufis and their ideas, noted that, as something perennial and sublime, it had no history as other things have a history. What he intends by that statement is to emphasise that the history of the Sufis is irrelevant compared to their perennial existence and function. What seems to many to be the 'history of the Sufis' is the half-understood debris of necessarily transient operations and activities.

So the Sufi fact is not easily to be regarded as an outgrowth of a culture, though Muslim Sufis have always insisted that its insights are both compatible with Islam and also constitute the inner dimensions of that and all other intact religions. This assertion, many people note, unexpectedly, has been widely accepted by members of several religions: by Jews, Hindus and Christians who have delved deeply into Sufism.

It is, of course, generally known that Sufi study and activity has mainly been developed and transmitted in the Islamic world, and that all the major public Sufi teachers have been within the Islamic fold. There is, however, abundant evidence which shows that Sufis have recognised the existence of Sufis far beyond the conventional frame of Islam. The position, in a literary sense, is further complicated by the fact that they have sometimes (as with Al-Ghazzali, who died in 1111 AD) been regarded as the most authoritative exemplars of Islamic theology, and yet at other times (as with Ibn Arabi the

* Hujwiri, *Kashf-al-Mahjub* (Revelation of the Veiled). Eleventh century.

Spaniard, who died in 1240 AD) as apostates and blasphemers. These conflicting opinions, of course, are nowadays seen to be reflections of observer bias much more than anything else.

EVOLUTIONARY RELIGION

These biases have been resolved in retrospect by the understanding that all authentic expressions of human spiritual aspiration may be seen as having a single source, and that the differences are in appearances only, imposed by cultural and local conditions. Thus, for instance, major religions are viewed from this standpoint as parts of a continuum of perception of needs culminating in the last world religion, Islam, dating from the seventh century of the Christian reckoning system.

Both Islamic ideology and Christian thinking, of course, would find no difficulty in the idea of the perenniality of religion; though few people seem able to keep this in their minds to any useful purpose. The Qur'an refers to believers in the *Jewish* dispensation, for instance, before Islam, as 'Muslims', and St Augustine himself said that Christianity existed before the time of the historical Jesus.

LITERALISTS AND PERCEPTIVES

The psychological problem which arose between Sufis and literalist theologian Muslims in the Middle Ages was very similar to the one which is also encountered in Christianity: the assumed conflict between religious belief and mystical perception. If faith and adherence to the Holy Law were the highest religious good, how could contact with the Infinite be needed, or even possible? If its purpose was to transcend the acceptedly complete spiritual dispensation of the Faith, was such a concept not dangerous elitism? If the consequences of such a pursuit put one man or woman above another in religious terms, what about the equality of all believers? What about the Church's hierarchy? Since in past times people were often judged for religious merit and 'goodness' only on their apparent *conduct*, surely, it was argued, those who believed in an allegedly more 'real' knowledge of the divine (as distinct from legal, ritual and social observance of an expression of it on Earth) were setting up an alternative hierarchy of merit: and a partly invisible, largely uncheckable one, at that?

This matter was thrashed out in the Middle Ages by both the Christian and Islamic theologians. In Christendom, mysticism was more severely dealt with, on the whole; partly because of the more centralised power of the Church, and partly because the Bible, unlike the Qur'an, did not seem to most of the theologians of the time to support the possibility of mysticism for independent individuals whose utterances were not verified by current dogma.

The Sufis could be judged by an enormous amount of what has even been called 'virtually the origin of modern psychological research and publication'. They pointed out, as we have noticed, that people's beliefs could be conditioned: and that they very often were. They insisted that hypocrisy could not be controlled by social legislation, however pious its source, and could only be transcended by self-realisation. They invoked passages in the Qur'an which supported the reality of individual knowledge of the Ultimate. To these contentions and to this contribution they added very much more; and this forms a most voluminous bibliography. Even Western scholars have been widely fascinated by this phenomenon: publishing one work on an average of every 14 days on Sufism in the past 200 years alone, in Western languages. The study of Sufi ideas, if not the deeper understanding of them, is thus of no new growth, even in the West.

It took the Sufis, however, nearly five centuries before they completely won acceptance for their teachings within Islam. That was about 800 years ago.

VERSATILITY OF SUFISM

During all this time, Sufis were sometimes canonised and sometimes judicially murdered; sometimes jeered at for flippancy – or for severity of behaviour. They have been described, too, by all the gradations in between these extremes. But throughout it, and subsequently, the repute of the Sufis was immensely reinforced by the production of literary classics in several major Eastern languages, and by the sustained emergence among them of astonishingly powerful, versatile, attractive and talented people. These were among the outward manifestations of inward development, according to the Sufis themselves, and in the eyes of many outside observers as well. It was to this extradimensional-perceptive source, too, that the enunciations of psychological insights, of facts of physics without what are today regarded as essential scientific apparatus, and other similar baffling affirmations of knowledge, to which I have referred, were ascribed.

Parallel with these events came several others. Sufi thought was adopted, as scholars of the time, and modern ones as well, have more than adequately demonstrated, by people from virtually all the cultures of a major portion of the then known world. There is, indeed, no other system of mystical thought on record which has been able to attract and recruit devout and iconoclastic thinkers from the Jewish, Christian and Hindu dispensations, effectively transcending the barriers of misunderstanding and ideological hostility which have certainly been as great as any others known to humanity.

Sufi ideas also penetrated the religious, secular and scientific writings and studies of the Middle East and Central Asia, as well as those of Europe, to an unprecedented extent. Certain Sufi teachers had droves of followers from religions other than Islam. And this is all a matter of uncontested, though often somewhat baffled, record.

At that time, of course, the present-day divisions of the academic disciplines and professions had not come about. Therefore, up to the late Middle Ages the Sufis, from Malaysia and the confines of China to Turkestan and India, and from Turkey to Arabia, Africa and Spain, continued their research and teaching in what we would nowadays call very many specialised fields. They worked and published in religion, in literature and poetry, in astronomy and physics, in community phenomena, and in psychological studies, these 'impractical and other-worldly iconoclasts', as one historian, somewhat baffled – and bafflingly – calls them.

THE APPROACH TO KNOWLEDGE

The Sufi approach to knowledge differs, however, dramatically from that of the European 'renaissance man', who excelled in all kinds of *chosen* interests. The Sufi's choice of worldly interests was, and is, held to be determined by his awareness of their *value* to the human race, in accordance with his perception of a cosmic design. His choice of study and activity is, to him, determined by *Sufi* understanding, not by arbitrary interest. Sufis do not cultivate interests and seek facts. They pursue successive layers of reality by understanding them. 'Experience without understanding is water without wetness.'

In modern, almost conversational, terms, the Sufi will say: 'Knowledge of absolute Truth transforms man. It is also this which puts everything else into perspective.' He can teach, if that is one of his functions (and many major historical Sufis would take no disciples), by virtue of the consciousness which enables him to know (a) himself; (b) the student; (c) how the student can be taught. The mere desire to teach is regarded as a disability rooted in ambition developing before understanding is mature.

DESIRE TO TEACH IS DISABLING

One major Sufi says: 'I had a desire to teach. I therefore ceased teaching until I became mature enough to do it properly, without the desire influencing my ability and therefore my duty to students. When the desire to teach left me, I started to teach.' Vocation-minded scholars, sentimentalists and others, of course, regard this quite tenable attitude with astonishment and even incredulity.

So, of course, the Sufi's ability to assess his pupil by personal capacity enables him to construct the study-course. If a Sufi is not a teacher, he exercises other functions in society, correspondingly determined: but that is an entirely different subject.

ATTUNEMENT

Since Sufi psychology involves the attunement of the Sufi with individual and collective humanity, and an equivalent attunement with an ultimate Reality, it is a harmonisation which can only come about after the 'practitioner' is 'trained'. Neither the practice nor the training, however, bears much

IDRIES SHAH

resemblance to anything understood by those words in other fields which we ordinarily encounter.

Sufism, therefore, is purposeful, and the purpose is, above all, *understanding*. In order to understand, one must enter a real Sufi study course: not just a familiarisation with the externals, which are in any case likely to have been superseded.

The Sufi must know himself before he can know others, in the sense and on the level on which Sufi psychology is held, by him, to function.

In dealing with Western-type thinkers, as in introducing *any* culture to unfamiliar concepts, we have to make sure that the following are among the procedures which we have employed:

There must be sufficient familiar content for the student to be able to build upon. This can be done with Sufi psychology by introducing the concepts, for instance, of flexibility, the inhibiting effect and self-indulgent consumerism of *undue* emotion, the frequent confusion of entertainment and study, so that the audience can think about these things. This is partly informational and partly designed to widen the horizon of the student's mind. One reason for the need for an ongoing relationship with students, of course, is that some of them will always seize upon one or more 'new' principles and imagine them to be a golden key. The world is full of people who have done this and have set up schools riveted onto the principles that, say, too much emotion is bad, or that quantity is better than quality, or the reverse. The imitativeness and premature operation – the *rush* to put something into action – is not confined to cargo-cults in New Guinea.

So 'anthropology – like charity – begins at home'. You may have observed it abroad, where the cargo-cult is conspicuous, but you can make a good deal of worthwhile use of it in any country, and above all in understanding neglected aspects of human thinking.

RATIONALISATION

Even the work on neglected aspects of human thinking has to be carefully monitored, such can be the bias in the culture towards fallacious interpretations: or self-indulgent, not fruitful, study; or perhaps it is only the old human nature taking over again.

I visited a commune a few weeks ago, and heard a very impressive, very loud, prayer being intoned and cried out by a suitably dressed suppliant who afterwards assured me that he was 'A Sufi'. So I asked him why he had been calling: 'God protect Joe, Bill, Mac, Lucie and Sanchez, and also Tickertac the dog…' with spasmodic and 'sincere' gestures and with such an expression of anxiety on his face, that I almost feared for his mental equilibrium. He was sweeping his hands and arms up and down as well, from time to time.

'Well, man, like, I've realised by what my Sufi teacher said recently that, like, I'm too selfish. But I *worry* that something might happen to me. So I've decided *not* to pray for myself, as that is selfish. But if I pray for everyone in this commune, including the dog, then if they are looked after, *I* will be too, since I *live here. Nothing* will harm me as long as I stick close to the others…' I am of course sure that he was not typical….

After mastery of the familiar content and the working of it in the mind of the recipient, we have to make sure that he will look at himself as well as at others, and see some of his traditional values in a new and extra light: in a *technical* light. You can sentimentalise, say, patience or self-effacement or service. If, on the other hand, you can see them *also* as things which enable one to learn, you can begin to get an idea of their additional *dynamic* – as distinct from their supposedly magical or demonstrably sentimental – functions.

In the course of these and other processes, you will surely attract people from all parts of the spectrum of humanity.

Because the mental stability of some of them depends on believing something to be true, those who think that you are denying this thing may oppose you. Because their mental stability or social integration depends on believing perhaps other things, those who think that you are reinforcing these will certainly love you. But this like and dislike is no part of Sufi activity.

In between all this, there is undoubtedly the unconscious attempt to manipulate things which continues, very strongly, working away in many otherwise quite unexceptionable minds, until they finally realise that this Sufi activity is not a matter of someone winning and someone losing, or of easy gains without effort: or of gains by randomly adopted forms of effort. In an entirely different context (interesting because it was in the awareness of the person concerned) I heard the other day of a conscious employment of situations very similar to what we get with would-be Sufis. A man told me that he wanted to find an apartment in Rome during a period when, for religious pilgrimage reasons, it was very difficult to do so.

The advertisement he put in the papers said: 'I am a sinner and hate my neighbours, but I urgently need an apartment for such-and-such a period in Rome.'

Although friends of his had previously advertised in vain, he was now inundated with replies from good God-fearing Italian folk who wanted to convert him or help him to wrestle with his sinfulness, presumably to gain some merit for themselves....This may be social or psychological manipulation, even religious activity. It has no place in Sufi operation.

Having got that out of the way, we can continue to the assertion that, since we are saying that what we think and do in Sufism is *never* at the expense of existing human character (but is rather more like a skill or other ability which may or may not, in action, indicate things about one's character which could change) we can claim to be working in the field of education rather than therapy, of higher psychology rather than entertainment, of understanding rather than belief.

I refer you to the mixture of assertion, demonstration, fact and practice, which make up the visible portion of the Sufi enterprise. Sufis are the bane of the formal thinker, because they will unhesitatingly break off a train of thought which could be channelled into a logical mode, if they think it necessary. They annoy scholars by asserting that Sufi literature and supposed dogmas are *operational*, not simply material to be made logical sense of in a linear manner; to torture out meanings from *all* writings, for everyone at any time, for example. They affront the overly sentimentalist, by holding fast to the claim that enough emotional stimulus is enough: even though none of them will ever deny that too little is undoubtedly insufficient for the good economy of the mind, body and community. It is mawkishness which is regarded as helping to prevent the understanding of higher things.

And so, every exposition of Sufi principles and practices, of Sufi thought and even its possible application to immediate concerns, must take place as part of a whole. That whole is the being of a Sufi, and to us the individual concepts and formulae (which so interest people who are trying to build general theories) are secondary, spin-offs, from something which is ultimately much more useful. Not only, be it noted, more useful, but something which makes the building of the general theory ultimately unnecessary, because the answers come holistically, and can actually be extrapolated from a single (though unrolled bit by bit) simple experience. Viewed from that perspective, working with the individual facts, like observation of how human minds work, collected and collated, is the *hard* way of doing things.

THE NATURAL AND THE SUPERNATURAL METHOD

There is a story about this. Don't stop me if you have heard it, for I think that it is one which can bear repetition. Come with me to a remote and – of course – mysterious and almost inaccessible fastness – where a Sufi is talking to a disciple. The student has just asked his teacher about the difference between various approaches to the acquisition of knowledge, since he wants to use his present abilities to delve into those which lie, for the moment, beyond him.

The Sage says: 'Yes, there *are*, of course, *two* possibilities of gaining higher knowledge, to penetrate and to transcend the barriers to understanding: to discharge the human duty. These are the *natural* method and the *supernatural*.'

'What is the natural one?' the student asks.

'The *natural* is the *Sufi* path: to pursue the study by its own methods, those which are traditional only because imposed by its source...'

'And the supernatural?'

'Oh, the supernatural – that would be if the academic and the scientific methods (as used in the West) were to obtain any results...'

As an Eastern psychology, however, Sufi practice sometimes seems unusual and difficult to people trained only in the either–or method of thought.

Jalaluddin Rumi put this attitude well when he stated that 'things which seem to be opposed may, in reality, be working together'. Here, I think, we do find a dramatic example of Eastern thinking: where *supposed* opposition may in fact operate as the reverse.

The principle is given human shape and set in the form of a tale in the East, in order to illustrate how we see social and psychological forces having an effect contrary to that intended by their originators, an effect which can be taken advantage of by the perspicacity of an objective observer.

BRIBERY

Mulla Nasrudin, the standard joke-figure who often appears in these stories, is about to engage in litigation, in this tale. He says to his lawyer: 'If I sent the judge 100 gold pieces, what effect would that have on his ruling in my case?'

The lawyer is horrified. 'You do that,' he says, 'and he'll find against you, for sure – you might even be arrested for attempted bribery!'

'Are you sure?'

'Quite sure, I *know* that judge.'

The case was heard, and the Mulla won.

'Well,' said the lawyer, 'you *did* get justice after all, you can't deny that...'

'Mind you,' said Nasrudin, 'the gold pieces also helped...'

'You mean you actually sent the judge *money*?' howled the lawyer.

'Oh yes,' said Mulla Nasrudin, 'but, of course, I sent the gold in the *other man's* name!'

Nasrudin is, of course, the device used here to show how things work – not an example of what someone should do under such circumstances. Sufi instructional tales are interpreted by people, in the study situation, in accordance with their growing ability to learn to recognise certain situations and their equivalence in human thought-systems and processes. A superficial thinker would imagine, for example, this only to be a tale of cunning and deception. But, as the Sufis say: 'You don't call a water-wheel cunning, claiming that it fools the river into giving up its water, do you?' The Sufis, in this sense, are technicians, and the instrumental function, at high levels of perception, is paramount.

The important thing is to be able to recognise what should be done and where and when it is indicated: not just to allow oneself to be pulled along by convention or by other people's assumptions.

The story of the 'real and artificial flowers', in one of its interpretations, shows the way to rethink a situation, and also how to put it into its proper area, and not to imagine that because people say that something is, say, spiritual, that it must therefore be so.

DEEP AND SHALLOW QUESTIONS

I think that this distinctly presents Sufi and non-Sufi psychology very well; and the way to treat the either–or ideas of crude assumptions, so as to leave room for *real* study.

Someone went to the public session of a wise man, with two bunches of flowers. He said:

'One of these bunches is of real flowers; the other, made with the greatest cunning in China, is artificial. If you are as perceptive as you are supposed to be, I would like you to tell me which is which. But you must not hold them very close, you must not smell or touch them.'

The sage said: 'A wise question is met with a wise answer, a shallow one with a shallow reply. This, however, is a horticultural one – bring a hive of bees!'

The bees, of course, chose the real flowers.

Here we have a glimpse of the kernel of Sufic participation-study, where people are being shown how to tell one thing from another: even how *hostile* observers can prepare themselves for eventually being able to understand Sufism. It is a million miles away from what we read in the tomes of some scholars, whom the Sufis so regularly castigate for restrictive study. The Sufi attitude to this is summed up in the phrase: 'The learner approaches the Teaching with the hope that it will always remain the same. The Teacher approaches the learner with the hope that this time he will be different.'

So the selection of people for working in Sufi psychology means not so much that they have qualities which control them, but that they have the ability to extend certain qualities at Sufistically important times, in varying places and situations. Particularly noteworthy in the Sufi enterprise is the *way* in which prevailing conditions are taken into account. Problems are no less regarded as to be surmounted as to be made use of. *Problem-solving*, to the Sufi, is only one out of several responses: they include preventing, avoiding and employing so-called problems.

It is concepts such as this which lie behind such apparently bewildering statements as:

> Nobody and no thing can stand between you and knowledge if you are fit for it; but anybody and anything can stand between you and knowledge if you are not fit for it.

One thing which Eastern and Western psychologies and cultures have in common is the insistence that human societies, in order to acquire, to concentrate and to pass on knowledge, require institutions through which this process can be carried out. Some things are learnt in schools, some in specialised institutes, some in universities; these are obvious examples. Linear and sequential thought is carried out in most such bodies, and the product will tend to be satisfactory for subjects which lend themselves to this treatment.

In Babylonia, very reputable institutions existed for the purpose of divining by means of marks on the entrails of animals; and even clay models of typical entrails were available to their distinguished scientists, for many centuries.

EFFICIENCY OF INSTITUTIONS

In parentheses one might note that these institutions, even in the modern world, are surprisingly often quite inefficient, many people not realising for a long time that they are. Perhaps the increasing criticisms of this kind of learning may lie behind some of today's desires to find other ways of study. A few weeks ago, as an example, I noticed that Professor Brian Griffiths, Chairman of the Joint Mathematical Council for the United Kingdom, said that '*Nobody*, of course, knows how *anyone* learns mathematics. But you can be sure it's *in spite of*, and *not because of*, the teacher.'*

As mathematicians may still have to improve or even devise new institutions for the teaching of their subject, it seems certain to me that people in the West interested in the work of Eastern workers in the mind–brain areas will eventually have to take note of the characteristic institutions through which we carry on our work. As to how soon and how effectively they can understand Sufism: it will depend on their own flexibility...

Now, all this – or much of it – may cause some people to think that Sufi studies, in their original form, cannot easily be operable in the Western atmosphere. I have to say that not only is Sufi activity possible, but that it is increasing.

I shall next deal with the main considerations which are applied in ensuring that such an institution can be viable in the modern world, so much of which is working on Western

* *Daily Mail*, London, 14 September 1976, p. 12, col. 5.

ideas anyway, whether it is geographically of the West or not. But, before doing that, it is perhaps a good idea to remind ourselves of the supply-and-demand mechanism on which this society functions.

There is always the possibility that things will start to work in a manner not intended for them to work, if the main objective is forgotten. No amount of demand for a 'Sufi hot-dog', say, will be likely to produce one.

Instead of there being as much ideological bias as formerly against really new forms of thought and study, we have now a little-noticed but widespread cultural phenomenon at work, which I would like to mention. In the process of trying to turn, say, parts of Indian philosophy into a psychologically – and hence culturally, in local terms – respectable pursuit, so much may be lost that we will have virtually none of the original vitality left. Dr Ornstein has called this 'the science of the East and the spirituality of the West' instead of the other way about.

There is an example of this tendency of the culture in a suitably neutral format which I noticed the other day in a newspaper report, to help us remember the consequences of one thing taking over another – and perhaps effectively extinguishing the first.

Not long ago, it seems, gasoline stations in North Italy began to sell red wine as well as gasoline. Now they are reporting that they are actually selling more *wine* than gasoline, to passing motorists.* Presumably, at some stage, the motorists will be too drunk to need any gasoline at all...This may be an analogy of the fate of Sufi ideas, introduced side by side with other kinds of study.

---

* *Sunday Telegraph*, London ('Mandrake'), 19 September 1976, p. 13 col. 6.

The current explosion of interest in the Sufi tradition clearly divides those who are attracted by what seems to them to be its strangeness and those who want to go into its psychology. Dr Leonard Lewin (in a recent article in the *International Philosophical Quarterly**) spoke of this being a period of one of those comparatively rare outpourings of Sufi knowledge, and welcomed this as an opportunity to profit from it. I am myself quite sure that the process is mutual. If, say, Western thinkers and psychologists had been prepared to do relatively objective research in Sufi ideas – which they were unable to do for cultural reasons and other priorities claiming their attention – they could have found, almost 1,000 years ago, literature full of remarkable and very 'modern' psychological ideas. But did they want to know about, say, conditioning, 1,000 years ago? After Pavlov and the Korean war, however, people began to look at our work... What stopped them before?

The exciting thing, from the Sufi point of view, is that we are now able to talk to a very wide variety of people prepared and willing to look at what we have been doing, within the structures and propositions which *we* have found to be necessary and adequate for their maintenance; and at a time when certain disabling biases are weakening. Equally, there still remain areas which Western-type thinkers have not yet shown an inclination to enter.

I want to give you a story now, which I hope (in addition to its other dimensions) may give some insight into the mutual incomprehensibility of East and West, which occurs when the only basis for interactions is by their respective assumptions,

* *IPQ*, Fordham, NY and Heverlee-Leuven (Belgium) Vol. XV, No. 3, pp. 353–64.

and if there is an absence of minimum information or perceptive capacity. I also think that it is quite funny.

THE MYSTIC SHRINE

This is a probably apocryphal story about a mystic shrine in, shall we say, Japan.

It was customary for pilgrims to make an offering of a few yen to the custodian, a monk, who sat there all day, mostly in contemplation.

A Western tourist, who nevertheless wished to have a proper respect for the proprieties, approached the holy place one day and, not knowing how much money to give, pulled out several thousand yen, which he offered to the monk. He was a little surprised when it was handed back to him with a smile and a shake of the head.

'I must have offered too little,' he thought, and, doubling the money, made his offering again.

The monk looked at the banknotes for a long moment. Then he shrugged and reached into a box and brought out an ancient scroll, which he presented to the visitor. And he walked away, down the road.

When translated, the mysterious document proved to be – the title-deeds to the shrine itself...

Although the Sufi institution is relative and short-term, designed to convey *experience* rather than itself to become more and more of an object of worship, and although Sufi exercises and concepts in the psychological sense exist, for the Sufi, for the purpose of transcending as well as using them, we can now talk to people in the West in this kind of language because we feel that they *have* started to direct their attention to perpetual change and development rather than to trying always to set up institutions whose power and authority are not matched by any essential and concurrent flexibility.

Because of this new frame of mind among contemporary people, following the breakdown of so many institutions which have been seen not to last as long as their originators imagined they would, and because scientists are now pretty sure that whenever you get to one point, there is another beckoning beyond it, the very psychology of psychologists can be seen to have changed. Check this, if you like, by reading published work in psychology over, say, the past 50 years.

And this is why we are able to indicate principles which are even more valuable as working hypotheses than as items of total belief – 'idols' as we call them – and can at last speak to people about structures which they may be prepared to see as means to ends, instead of merely as ends in themselves.

VII Involvement in Sufi Study

WHEN WE TALK about the possibilities of involvement in Sufi activity, we must have a very clear idea that the possibilities are inextricably linked with the desires of the person involved. If you are looking for something to make you feel better, or to make you feel significant, or to assuage your need for togetherness – you will look for something which offers these things. But you will not be involved with Sufis or in the Sufi activity. *And* you will have forgotten that there is a perfectly good American phrase saying 'There *is* no such thing as a free lunch.'

It is here in the West that one would very much like to understand how things have deteriorated, and would like to prove the inaccuracy of the now famous gibe: 'Spirituality was born in the Near East, developed in Central Asia, grew old in Iran, went mad in Europe – and travelled to America to die!'

In matters like these, although far from a purist, I am a supporter of the French proverb: 'There is no such thing as a *fairly good* omelette!'

Let us recapitulate how the Sufis *do* see their activity:

What most people call 'Sufism' is traditionally known in the East as 'being a Sufi', or 'The Sufiyya', and the 'ism' part is very typically a Western concept. If we speak of 'Sufism', it is only for ease of communication. In a similar way, a citizen of Wales will call himself *Welsh* – even though this is an Old English word meaning 'foreigner'.

Its purpose is to enable us to understand what lies behind ordinary limitations of perception. This is referred to both as experiencing Reality and as realising one's potential. These studies, involving the capacity of encountering what is beyond humanity, are quite distinct from the inculcation of an ideology or training in and eliciting habitual responses. When we talk of this enterprise as a psychology, we must remember that it covers areas far beyond the usual meanings assigned to this term at the present time in the West.

THE PATH

The Sufi system is pursued by the organisation of groups of people. Linked to a central direction, to form a community which is based on principles and realities beyond the herd-instinct or the pleasures obtained through belonging to something. This enterprise is called the *Tarika*, the Path. Far from being characterised by constant activity and perpetual teaching, it is just as concerned with such recondite statements as: 'To be neglected by a man of wisdom is better than to gain the total attention of a fool.'

The *Tarika* embodies action and inaction, learning and teaching, in a rhythm which concentrates and stabilises it into an institution with the necessary flexibility and sophistication. Its action has been referred to as being by means of *Baraka*, a subtle communications and enrichment element. In deteriorated, folkloric and lower-level thinking, this 'substance' (as it has been termed) has been imagined to be something in the nature of magical power. In quasi-scientific thought, it is sometimes conceived as a force with special characteristics like, say, magnetism. Such characterisations, for the Sufi, succeed only in illustrating the limitations of both kinds of formulation, not in defining this element at all. In reality it is only 'understood' by most people through their misunderstanding, their distortion, of it.

THE WESTERN SEEKER

We can conveniently remember in this connection the tale of
the man who heard a word and assumed it meant something,
and after that was able to 'understand' as he thought, another
statement which contained the word, but which did not mean
that at all:

In Kabul, Afghanistan, they tell the story of a foreign Seeker-
after-Truth. As soon as he got down from his aeroplane, he
asked an engineer, in a foreign language:

'Who is the greatest Sufi Teacher?'

The man, not understanding, said: '*Namifahmam*', which
means 'I don't understand you'.

But, of course, the visitor thought that this was the name
of the great man whom he was seeking.

Shortly afterwards, he saw a crowd watching a funeral
procession.

'Who is being buried?' he asked a bystander.

'*Namifahmam*,' said the man – 'I don't understand you.'

'To think that I arrived too late to see him,' cried the Seeker,
and returned sorrowfully to his own country.

Now this man tells anyone who will listen of his great
pilgrimage and its poignant end.

DO THE IGNORANT UNDERSTAND THE WISE?

The essence of the Sufi operation's success is to give, rather
than to want to get, to serve, rather than to be served.
Although almost all cultures pay lip-service to this as an ideal,
the failure really to operate it means that the mental, the psychological, posture which unlocks the greater capacity of the
consciousness is not achieved where this element is lacking,
and so people do not learn. You can't cheat in this game.

It is often considered a paradox, especially by people who want to get something and to rationalise their greed as, at least, laudable ambition, that when the ambition is suspended anything can be gained. The easiest way of dealing with this is to affirm, with relative truth, that since people customarily want too much, the non-ambitious posture is a corrective, which enables them to be just ambitious enough and not too greedy: focussing their mentation to operate correctly in this respect. Sufi mentors are only too well aware of the underlying greed and how and why it must be assuaged:

'The wise,' it is said, 'understand the ignorant, for they were themselves once ignorant. But the ignorant do not understand either themselves or the wise, never having been wise themselves.' This is certainly true in the matter of due and correct measure in Sufi matters.

TWO KINDS OF SUFI GROUP

Among the legitimate Sufis, those with an intact tradition, there are two kinds of study-groups where the basic work is done. These are:

1. Associations of people trying to find out if they can form, maintain and stabilise a group with potential. These are usually known as 'dervish groups'. Among the tests are whether the group will deteriorate into a power-system or a hierarchical set-up; whether the activities of the group will degenerate into a mere search for personal satisfactions (since social satisfactions can, of course, be obtained anywhere else), or whether some other kind of immature demand will develop. Very many such groups are not successful, since their members, by a sort of unsensed

conspiracy, seldom recognise how easily subjective demands can take over and under how deep a disguise they may operate. Many of the collections of spiritual people which one sees in the West, and not a few in the East, are really this kind of group. Stabilised they may be: spiritual activities they are not.

2. Sufic groups, called *Taifas*, are either established by a teacher or accepted by him (or her) from among individuals or members of the first type of group, supposing that they have avoided the preliminary pitfalls. They often have a keynote or outward function, as well as an inner and developmental one. This may mean that their members could be engaged in art, social action, human service, even commerce, as well as carrying out appropriate exercises and studies. The purpose of these outward activities includes testing whether the people can work successfully in an organic whole without (a) subjective considerations ruining their operation, or (b) the outward activity being taken over and being 'spiritualised' by people imagining that, say, social service is sacred instead of a minimum duty.

In both Eastern and Western communities it is not rare to find the derivatives of such groups where one or the other activities has gained the ascendancy. Groups which concentrate only upon spiritual exercises, concentration, contemplation or meditation are, diagnostically, this kind of deteriorated group. The exercises have become the 'commerce' of the group, and its social expression.

Secondary materials, including art works, poetry, literature and artefacts, have traditionally, though not uniquely, originated from such groups. This reputable origin has had the further complicating effect of causing well-meaning imitators, often very pious but essentially superficial ones, to examine and attach themselves to the secondary materials, with correspondingly poor results in terms of real understanding, though not necessarily in personal satisfactions.

When this happens, it is either the 'greed industry' at work, or the group being used for psychotherapeutic or social stability purposes. If you are one of the people who want to eat their cake and have it, you would qualify for this phase of such a group.

Someone was telling me the other day that his opinion was that one of the great triumphs of Western man had been to divert human greed into a thirst for knowledge, in a sufficient number of cases to make education and human progress a major achievement.

This may look, at first glance, like a great thought. But if you want to believe this, you must close your eyes to research done centuries ago which determined that you can only learn a few things by such a method, and that when you get to a blind-alley through trying this approach, you may find yourself asking people who have done the research what went wrong with your programme...

GREED AND ASPIRATION

How do you transform, say, human greed into a laudable motivation for progress? Quite obviously, you can channel a certain amount of energy into constructive places only when you know what you are dealing with, and how to deal with it. The solution which has, as anyone can see, usually been attempted, is to reiterate constantly: 'Don't be greedy – be constructive.' Anyone can also see how this puts at a premium the ability to conceal greed under a constructive-looking façade.

Instead of assuming that greed is normality, one should see it as an abnormality. Beside it lies normality, trying to find expression.

So all human groups, unless carefully monitored, are subject to 'spiritual deterioration' when the objective is obscured and finally eliminated through the overdevelopment of easier-to-follow activities like prayer, or discipline, and so on. People talk, almost endlessly it sometimes seems to me, about 'learning wisdom from experience'. Among the Sufis, however, people learn from experience how to *recognise* wisdom. Experience is useless unless there is a means to digest it.

The great variety of esoteric groups with differing outward appearances is a result, according to Sufi assessment, of only two factors. The first is that temporary teaching-frames suited to a specific community have later been adopted as sacrosanct; the second is that the secondary activities have become oversimplified into supposed essentials.

Doctrinal differences do not exist in Sufi understanding, since all perceptions of truth are the same; hence such differences belong to the level of ideologically based, not experience-tested, systems. Ideologies exist only where there is no absolute knowledge. If you know something, you do not have to believe or disbelieve it....

Ideology is associated with automatism; doctrine, in the Sufi sense, with the instrumental. It is both natural and hazardous to confuse current preoccupations, or even perennial questions, with eternal truths. Truth is what you can learn, not what you think you must learn. It is what is there, not what you want to be there. March towards a landmark, by all means, the Sufi says: there is often no other way of keeping to the shortest route. But when you do this, you must also know that this is an activity to a purpose. The landmark and perhaps the habit of marching must be thrown aside when it has served its purpose. Those who can understand this, and live with it, can become Sufis.

Even if I wanted to do so, I could not forget how grotesque things can become in this area. I have seen it so often; but I will tell you the most advanced case of it I know, for illustrative purposes:

THE BALANCED EGG

I was challenged by a reverend member of a certain spiritual community to balance an egg on the tip of my nose. This, I was told, had been successfully done by a former Head of their teaching, and not very long ago, at that.

Since I couldn't do it, I was regarded, though temporarily I am glad to report, by the others present, as spiritually inadequate. This impression was not dispelled, to put it no higher, by my devout challenger.

The spell was broken by a dissident in the group, the equivalent to the child in the crowd, who said:

'This seems to me heroic but hazardous, and elegant but essentially materialistic; to say nothing of the danger I sense, in such activities, of falling a victim to the sin of pride.'

In conversation, later, with a prominent, but retired, leader of this community, I asked him how the egg-trick had started.

'It was originally devised,' he told me, 'for television.'

*   *   *

The true group, the kind known as 'organic', is developed – indeed, comes into being – in response to the potentialities of a situation.

Of course it is not always possible to convey these facts to everyone, however much people say: 'Tell it like it is.'

You have to temporise, generally because many people cannot take all this in at one gulp – especially if they have come to hear something else. (Such as that they can obtain something they don't know about by methods that have never worked.)

'COME BACK IN THREE YEARS'

One day when I was very young, I was sitting in the company of a renowned Sufi master.

A traveller had come in, having journeyed for many months to see our Sufi.

'I have come because I am sure that I must ask you now to accept me as a pupil,' he said.

The Sufi answered: 'Come back in three years and have no contact with me in the meantime.'

As the visitor withdrew, I gasped at the length of time given, and the hardship of the 'prescription'.

'Yes, I know,' said the Sufi, 'I should have said "ten years" – but I did not want him to think that I was harsh. It would do *him* no good to have something against *me*.'

IMPORTANCE OF THE ORGANISATION

Since the manifestation of the higher human perception and its stabilisation are so relatively difficult in social and professional environments which constantly drive people towards exaggerated ambition, fear, display, habit, and so on, the maintenance and integrity of the instrument is of the utmost importance. This, the *Tarika*, is therefore regarded as the 'real home', and the school and source of stimulus and protector of the student in matters of Sufi studies. In decayed systems, as we have seen, the container is mistaken for the content, and organisation-worship (traditionally termed by Sufis 'idolatry') supervenes.

The degree of realisation of the individual and of the group depend upon the harmony of the knowledge introduced by the direction, with the protection of the individual from extremes on the one hand, and his own sincerity and preparedness to align himself with truth – not bias or dogma or the craving for instant or ready satisfactions – on the other. 'The degree of potentiality depends on the correctness of one's aspiration.'

SIMILARITY OF THIS APPROACH TO OTHER FORMULATIONS

Attention to the above points will show that they are close to the requirements of some very much more familiar teaching situations. No vocational enterprise, for instance, could operate without a source of teaching, suitable students grouped in the appropriate place at the right time, a minimum of essential information and certain conduct, and the avoidance of distractions and irrelevancies. Certain kinds of effort are also necessary to the attainment of any objective. In both the East and West, as we have noted, people are accustomed to numerous organisations through which their aspirations may find expression and, it is hoped, fulfilment. The Sufi institution of the *Tarika* is such an instrument. But it is not going too far to say that the attraction of 'esoteric' studies, for many people, lies exactly in the *lack* of order and purpose in vestigial and other forms. The Sufis, in common with people in all other purposeful undertakings, maintain their own frameworks and organisations.

This is one reason why Sufic activity is said to have 'no history'. Not being historiocentric, Sufic attention regards history, personality, 'esoteric tourism' and 'museum-keeping' activities as ancillary at best and not ever as central. The Sufi's relevance and effectiveness is constantly refreshed from its source, through the Sufi organism, not by reference to static lumps of doctrine or frozen ritual. Counterfeit gold, as Rumi said, is made only because there is such a thing as real gold for people to try to imitate.

OTHER 'HIGHER CONSCIOUSNESS' GROUPINGS

The exponents of Sufi study do not ordinarily pronounce upon matters such as the genuineness or otherwise of specific individuals, cults or schools. Like any other legitimate teaching body, they are responsible to state their principles and to maintain the integrity and progress of the activity in which they are engaged. This does not imply competing with bodies which prefer to operate on different bases. Enquirers, however, should be able to assess such other entities as they encounter, should they wish to do so, by reference to the schemata of the correct Sufi tradition, openly available, and by the application of common sense. 'A dog and a cat may fight to decide which of them is a rat. A Sufi is more concerned with the truth.'

RANDOM ADOPTION OF 'TEACHINGS'

The fact that some Sufi and other teaching material is available in general-circulation books has produced two effects: (1) Some people familiarise themselves with the material, and then approach legitimate Sufi sources if they wish to enter into comprehensive studies. This is, of course, one purpose of the publications mentioned. (2) Others, who are probably in the majority, but whose efforts are insubstantial, attempt to employ the materials to teach themselves or others, while lacking the essential experiences upon which alone such teaching functions can be productively sustained. Their enthusiasm or ambition outruns their preparedness to learn correctly. We have noted the consequences: and you can see them everywhere.

The parallel with more familiar learning systems can usefully be invoked again here. The random-adopters may be said to be doing themselves and others as much good as people who know nothing about medical science would if they were to read a few books and buy a few medicaments. 'Truth seeks you totally. Make sure that you really seek it.'

PATTERN OF THE SUFI ENTERPRISE

The Sufi enterprise is carried out in the following pattern:

1. Materials are circulated from a source of knowledge;
2. Individuals and groups familiarise themselves with this material;
3. Those who seek instant satisfactions, attractive theory, and so on, are discouraged;
4. People needing comprehensive study enter into it;
5. Outward and inward activities, in individuals and groupings, are organised. These are based on assessed needs and possibilities;
6. The appearance of the effort may or may not have a visible affinity with a superseded framework, however attractive;
7. Individuals and groupings are harmonised by a programme of interaction between them and the guiding element, also referred to in some aspects as a

'central direction'. During this process, conditions are established and maintained for genuine Sufic activity, which involves including the necessary 'nutrients' and avoiding limiting factors.

8. Those people and groupings which have preferences for other kinds of association are given early and adequate opportunities to appreciate that their requirements have to be fulfilled elsewhere, to the contentment of all. Each will then be able to follow a path consistent with his or her true current aim and capacity.

As a psychology, one Sufi procedure can be isolated to make sense of people and situations which, if one adopts customary methods, remain insusceptible to analysis.

Ordinary human assessment is generally based upon looking for outstanding characteristics in people, and labelling them with this as their 'behaviour-pattern'.

It is more than just interesting, however, to observe that these assumed outstanding characteristics reflect what the person is like.

They do, in fact, reflect certain results of learnt behaviour.

Many years ago, a Sufi sage advised me to look at the behaviour of people – shall we say including tolerance, indifference, hostility and the rest – and then to disregard these and to look for even more, less well-defined behaviours.

I was amazed, when I developed the knack of doing this, to discover whole new and unfamiliar ranges of purposeful behaviour in people, signalling parts of the total behaviour, which enabled me to make sense of the whole, in a way which isolating only the crude and socially conditioned expressions of behaviour did not.

This is, of course, an advanced way of what we all term 'not being distracted by appearances' or not generalising from too little material. Transformed into an observation technique, it becomes a truly remarkable assessment tool.

But I will end with a phrase which my first teacher used to say – and from which I learnt more than from anything else which I can register – from the voluminous and ancient lore of the Sufis, and which is a key, if there ever was one, to the method of understanding this astonishingly rich wisdom:

> HE is a Master who may teach without it being
> totally labelled teaching;
> HE is a student who can learn without being
> obsessed by learning.

VIII   Conclusion

THE AREA OF psychological activity in the human being is for the Sufi that of his secondary, raw and conditioned self. This is not the self which achieves higher consciousness, but is the socially operative one. Customary human efforts are directed towards stabilising this secondary self and integrating it in society (whether a religious or other society), and the emotional experiences which are possible to this self are generally confused with higher experiences, giving rise, at best, to therapy or the formation of a new tribe or society (actually a cult), not to a body of more aware people. I say at best because this is the best that can be achieved when working on this level; not to indicate that this is not to be desired. But people who need therapy or a tribe should attend to this need first, and should not confuse it with higher perceptions.

There is a Sufi saying that: 'None attains to the Ultimate Truth until a thousand honest people have called him an infidel.' This holds good, too, in the secular world, including that part of the world which concerns itself with psychology and metaphysics.

In order that the Sufi understanding of the human mind may be displayed and experienced, even in our highly sophisticated present-day world, certain myths must be set aside, certain taboos ignored. One of these is that social harmony and higher experiences are the same or similar or lead one to the other. Now the fact is that social harmony and mental balance are essentials, just like food or other nutritions. But to glamorise these things and to distort their functions is to show lack of knowledge.

We are living in a world where honesty and the correct assessment of situations often seems like insanity, at best like humour.

This is the area in which our basic data, our premises, have to be questioned: is the consciousness with which we are familiar the same as that which might be raised higher? Is mental stabilisation or social comfort another word for being on the way to Heaven or is it a lower though very essential herd-need? What are the elements, if any, which have to be worked with in order to understand more of human capabilities in the realm of the mind? Can we, in an analytically-based society, really dare to analyse the things which we, like most herd-minded communities, take as constants, including whether those who want to teach or to carry on research are fitted for it, in respect of being able to ask the right questions and being able to profit from the answers? Are the people of the modern world so obsessed by modernism that they believe that they can take apart traditional systems and remake them in a more viable form than they already are?

And I have not even begun to ask the questions which a Sufi would ask if he were to be faced with someone who wanted to know about his teaching...

Sufi applications are the application of knowledge already gained by the people who have gained it. It is not the carrying on of age-old customs or even the moving from one piece of discovered information to the next. The assertion, by the Sufi, that he has not only travelled this way before but therefore knows best the unique way to retrace his steps with his students, is not negotiable. For students, almost by definition, display the tendencies, even in their attempts to analyse, which the Sufi knows bring ignorance (obsession, lower-level amusements and so on) and not knowledge.

So, although the present interest in Sufi work of the past is welcome, the only thing which can be said in answer to the attempt to relate it to the present is to state, in the nicest way allowed by prevailing conditions, that the tradition and methodology is as always, intact, alive and well. And that Sufis will always share it, without any reservations, with whomever wishes to approach it in the only way in which most ancient and still valid experience has shown it to be approachable: by means of the methods which the higher knowledge itself indicates to be effective.

Some Further Reading

Burke, O. M., *Among the Dervishes*, London: Octagon, 1973; New York: E. P. Dutton Inc., 1975.

Deikman, A., PhD, *Personal Freedom: On Finding your Way to the Real World*, New York: Grossman/Viking Press, 1976.

Deikman, A. J., MD, *Sufism and Psychiatry*, Journal of Nervous and Mental Disease, 165, 5, 1977 (pp. 318–29).

Lewin, L., PhD, *Sufi Studies: East and West*, International Philosophical Quarterly, XV, 3, 1975 (pp. 353–64).

Ornstein, R. E., PhD, *The Psychology of Consciousness*, San Francisco and Reading, 1972; New York and London (new edition) 1978, Academic Press.

Pendlebury, D. (translator) *The Walled Garden of Truth*, London: Octagon, 1974; New York: E. P. Dutton, 1976.

Shah, Idries *Learning How to Learn*, London: Octagon, 1978.

The Elephant in the Dark, London: Octagon, 1974 (Geneva University Lectures).

Special Illumination, London: Octagon, 1978.

Neglected Aspects of Sufi Study, London: Octagon, 1978 (New School for Social Research lectures, New York).

Williams, L. F. Rushbrook (editor) *Sufi Studies East and West*, London: Octagon with Jonathan Cape, 1974; New York: Dutton, 1973.

LEARNING HOW TO LEARN

'*Learning How to Learn* is both the distillation of a million words and a guide to the whole body of the Shah materials. Certain irresistible keys keep the reader on the edge of the seat...A book which surely marks a watershed in studies of the mind.'

> *Psychology Today* Choice of the Month

'Bracing and often shocking. Shah's approach can best be described as a brisk and informed commonsense at its highest level.'

> *Books and Bookmen*

'Packed with important information.'

> *New Society*

THE HUNDRED TALES OF WISDOM

Tales, anecdotes and narratives used in Sufi schools for the development of insights beyond ordinary perceptions, presented by Idries Shah, and translated from the Persian. Traditionally known as 'The Hundred Tales of Wisdom' the stories are of the life, teachings and miracles of Jalaluddin Rumi from Aflaki's *Munaqib*, together with certain important tales from Rumi's works.

SPECIAL ILLUMINATION: THE SUFI USE OF HUMOUR

Idries Shah is well known for his publishing of the Nasrudin corpus of teaching stories, in which humour is used to display human behaviour and also to engage the mind in a different manner. 'Special Illumination' is the phrase used by the great teacher and mystic Jalaluddin Rumi to stress the importance of humour in metaphysical experience.

> 'Many jokes in *Special Illumination* are collected from or set in the west ... he demonstrates that we have perhaps failed to appreciate, or even notice, our own instructional riches.'
>
> *New Society*

NEGLECTED ASPECTS OF SUFI STUDY

Based on university lectures, *Neglected Aspects of Sufi Study* deals with many of the problems of Sufi methods of study, those that is which militate against its effective progress in the modern world...notably the unrecognised assumptions which we make about ourselves and about learning and its processes.

This book provides a companion to the twenty volumes of Sufi studies and literature which Shah has extracted from the literature and practice of Sufis over the past one thousand years.

> 'It elaborates points found particularly difficult in our culture because of sets of mind.'
>
> *Books and Bookmen*

A VEILED GAZELLE: SEEING HOW TO SEE

As the great mystic Ibn Arabi explains in his *Interpreter of Desires*, 'A Veiled Gazelle' is a subtlety, an organ of higher perception.
Sufi experientialists refer to the activation of these centres of awareness as the awakening of real knowledge of Truth beyond form.
This book deals with the symbolical and instrumental employment in Sufi studies of its literature: which is seldom didactic and never meant only as entertainment, although regarded in all cultures as some of the world's greatest writing.

THE SUFIS

'Many forlorn puzzles in the world, which seemed to suggest that some great spiritual age somewhere in the Middle East had long since died and left indecipherable relics, suddenly come to organic life in this book.'
                    Ted Hughes: The Listener

'Sufism is…"the inner secret teaching that is concealed within every religion". The book has flashes of what (without intending to define the word) I can only call illumination.'
                    D. J. Enright: New Statesman

'Fully authoritative' (*Afghanistan News*); 'Important historically and culturally' (*Los Angeles Times*); 'Incredibly rich in scope and fine detail' (*Psychology Today*); 'The definitive statement of Sufism' (*Library Journal*); 'Now its influence is spreading where long overdue' (*The American Scholar*); 'More extraordinary the more it is studied' (*Encounter*); 'Most comprehensively informative' (*New York Times Book Review*).

THE TALE OF THE FOUR DERVISHES
OF AMIR KHUSRU
RETOLD BY AMINA SHAH

This allegory was recited when he was ill to the great thirteenth century Sufi teacher Nizamuddin Awliyya by his disciple Amir Khusru, the eminent Persian poet. On his recovery, Nizamuddin placed a benediction on the book, and it is widely believed that the recitation of this story will restore health to the ailing. The allegorical dimensions it contains are part of a teaching-system which prepares the mind for spiritual enlightenment.

Since the tale was translated into Urdu a century-and-a-half ago, it has been regarded as a classic of that language. Amina Shah's present re-telling of it now enables its beauty and power to reach the English-speaking world.

'An entertaining book...I can't imagine anyone not enjoying this book's atmosphere and friendly charm, where the voice of the traditional story-teller can be heard behind every line.'

Doris Lessing in *Books and Bookmen*

TEACHINGS OF RUMI:
THE MASNAVI
TRANSLATED & ABRIDGED BY
E. H. WHINFIELD

Jalaluddin Rumi was born in Balkh (Afghanistan) in 1207 and died in 1273 at Konia, in Asiatic Turkey. His great work, *The Masnavi*, was forty-three years in the writing. During the past seven hundred years, this book, called by Iranians 'The Qur'an in Persian', a tribute paid to no other book, has occupied a central place in Sufism. Rumi's name is associated with the founding of the Order known in Europe as the 'Dancing Dervishes', and in the East as 'The Path of the Master'.

'*The Masnavi* is full of profound mysteries, and a most important book in the study of Sufism – mysteries which must, for the most part, be left to the discernment of the reader.'

F. Hadland Davis

'Rumi was not only a poet and mystic and the founder of a religious order: he was also a man of profound insight into the nature of man.'

Professor Erich Fromm

A Request

If you enjoyed this book, please review it on Amazon and Goodreads.

Reviews are an author's best friend.

To stay in touch with news on forthcoming editions of Idries Shah works, please sign up for the mailing list:

 http://bit.ly/ISFlist

And to follow him on social media, please go to any of the following links:

 https://twitter.com/idriesshah

 https://www.facebook.com/IdriesShah

 http://www.youtube.com/idriesshah999

 http://www.pinterest.com/idriesshah/

 http://bit.ly/ISgoodreads

 http://idriesshah.tumblr.com

 https://www.instagram.com/idriesshah/

http://idriesshahfoundation.org